C000136644

Staging Cities

Act 1
Concrete & Ink

Storytelling and the Future
of Architecture

Edited by
Marta Michalowska and
Justinien Tribillon

Act 1

Concrete & Ink

Storytelling and the Future of Architecture

Contents

Introduction

concrete

    noun 1. a building material made from a mixture of broken stone or gravel, sand, cement, and water, which can be spread or poured into moulds and forms;
           2. a mass resembling stone on hardening.

  adjective 1. existing in a material or physical form; not abstract;
           2. denoting a material object as opposed to an abstract quality, state, or action.

ink

    noun 1. a coloured fluid or paste used for writing, drawing, printing, or duplicating.

    verb 1. mark (words or a design) with ink;
           2. cover (type or a stamp) with ink before printing;
           3. obliterate something, especially writing, with ink.

storytelling

    noun 1. the activity of writing, telling, or reading stories;
           2. the art of telling stories.

future

    noun 1. a period of time following the moment of speaking or writing; time regarded as still to come;
           2. events that will or are likely to happen in time to come;
           3. the likely prospects for or fate of someone or something in time to come;
           4. a prospect of success or happiness.

architecture

    noun 1. the art or practice of designing and constructing buildings;
           2. the style in which a building is designed and constructed, especially with regard to a specific period, place, or culture;
           3. the complex or carefully designed structure of something.

Stories are, and have been, part of all cultures around the world: from myths to TV series, from fables to radio plays, from epic poems to theatre, from novels to films, from oral histories to video games. Fictional stories have the power to sweep one into a different world, at times to a vision of the future or distant past. And, just like buildings, stories are constructed. In a novel for instance, there is an intricate maze of layers of time, narrative points of view with their circles of consciousness and shifts, a psychic distance between a narrator and their characters, the internal and the external. When seamlessly pulled together, these narrative structures are at the service of the story and don't draw attention to themselves, enabling one to enter a constructed world. In a similar way, in a city or building, one perhaps rarely questions the height of a ceiling in a foyer of an office block or the width of an underpass connecting two sides of a road. One inhabits the space created and mostly accepts the construct that makes one move in a certain way, see a particular vista, become alert, relaxed or uncomfortable without unpicking the elements that generate emotions, reactions or behaviours.

At the same time, stories are deployed at every stage of the planning and design of cities and buildings: from the narratives underpinning regeneration projects to sales brochures for new flats and offices. Narratives can be put to work to present a particular vision or to persuade. They can become latent, taking the form of prejudice, racism, exclusion or oppression. They may pretend to be facts while reflecting distorted reality. They may be meticulously constructed or emerge through hearsay. They may be created to serve a particular ideology or set of social or political goals. They may be based on false premises and assumptions, either conscious or unconscious. They may take a sweeping, top-down view similar to an omniscient narrator in a novel or short story, or may choose to get closer to those on the ground and their experience, offering a perspective similar to a close-third-person narration. Perhaps planners, developers or architects are not always entirely aware that storytelling forms part of their practice, and they do not fully examine the way in which they use narrative structures to construct stories that get buildings built or demolished.

Planners, architects and engineers operate within a wider culture steeped in stories that permeate all aspects of life. Those that design cities and buildings watch films and TV series, listen to the radio, podcasts and gossip from their friends and neighbours, and read newspapers and books. They are not beyond urban myths and political ideology. They respond to the world around them, and form views and perspectives that inevitably influence their work and the choices they make.

At Theatrum Mundi, we explore how the arts could offer different ways for city-makers – architects, engineers and urban planners – to examine the practices of designing and redesigning cities and their elements: streets, public spaces, transport links or buildings. This is the first book in the series *Staging Cities* that across four volumes proposes a shared space, bringing together constellations of knowledge and approaches from across storytelling, choreography, sound and lighting design, and city-making to search for points of crossover, overlaps and perhaps common ground and understanding in creating, designing and living *city-ness*.

Concrete and Ink: Storytelling and the Future of Architecture looks at cities and specific buildings or places within them through storytelling. We were interested in the ways in which cities, streets, estates, houses and public buildings can be narrated through, mostly, fictional stories. How can they be constructed, reconstructed or deconstructed through storytelling? Who tells the story? Is the narrator reliable or unreliable? What is the worldview of the narrator or the characters? Who are the characters? What is their relationship to the city, the building or the place, as well as to each other? Is the city or the building a setting or a character in the story? What are the objectives of the narrator and the characters, and what obstacles do they encounter along the way?

We were particularly interested in looking at the future and how writers, as well as game designers and animators, construct visions for what is to come or examine past futures of cities and buildings. The extremes of utopia and dystopia seem to hold a gravitational power over imagination of the future. They both avoid a multi-layered perspective where positive and negative elements are in flux and overlap. Ultimately, one person's utopia may be another person's dystopia, and those can shift over time, or coexist in different spheres of life and experience. What is fascinating about utopia and dystopia is their divergence from reality: the gap between the perception and the state of things, between the assumptions and the actual conditions, the wishes and the facts. We asked the writers we commissioned to tread the line between the two seductive edges of projection into what's to come.

Further into the future of our exploration of the overlaps between storytelling and architecture and urban planning, we would be interested to see how fictional storytelling could offer a set of alternative methods to examine plans for development or redevelopment of cities: through creating a set of characters and *letting* them inhabit the proposed places over a *longer* fictional time. This approach could bring into the proposed places characters with a broader range of lifestyles, viewpoints, experiences and behaviours that may stray from cut-out-like *average* models of humans and, thus, play a role in foreseeing and identifying areas that may need to be reconsidered.

Concrete and Ink: Storytelling and the Future of Architecture could have been a collection of essays or an academic study analysing the crossovers of storytelling with architecture and urban planning, but we opted to address these questions through commissioning writers to respond with stories. Our aim was to use storytelling to take our readers, you, into the words presented by the writers and let you experience the architecture and urban planning within them first hand without mediation or guidance from us.

The stories in this collection offer an encounter with: a house on the outskirts of Lagos kept from sinking below the ground by stories in **Ben Okri's *The House Below***; a city requiring a complete shift in understanding of the boundary between nature and architecture in **Sophie Mackintosh's *Wild City***; an enormous slab block designed to sway in the wind where bath water sloshes in **Alison Irvine's *Red Road Stories***; an oasis garden on the top of a condemned tower block which nurtures an unexpected friendship in **Matthew Dooley's** graphic short story ***The Tower***; a new town and its negative double in **Nina Leger's *The Life and Death and Life of Antipolis***, translated from French by **Natasha Lehrer**; a communist-era national stadium in Warsaw built with rubble of the city's wartime ruins in **Marta Michalowska's *Minor Characters***; a city subjected to an onslaught on its culture in **Adania Shibli's *Word War***, translated from Arabic by **Mona Kareem**; a shopping mall in Santiago that is the site of choice for those looking to end their lives in **Alia Trabucco**

Zerán's *The Blind Spot*, translated from Spanish by **Sophie Hughes**; an iconic building of a museum under siege in **Bedwyr Williams' *The Militia***; the CERN straddling the border between Switzerland and France, as well as between science and politics, in **Crystal Bennes' *CERN: A Scientific Utopia***. Two interviews looking at the intersection between storytelling, place and time in game design and animation complete this volume: ***Of Time Mechanics & Oxytocin*** with **Jodie Azhar** and ***In Between Frames*** with **Meghana Bisineer.**

Storytelling is a two-way process. Receiving stories is as much an act of storytelling as telling or writing them: both sides are needed for the process to take place, and each makes a unique contribution that lets stories offer different worlds through the eyes and minds of their characters, who may entertain, provide escape, share their knowledge and experience, challenge, frighten, touch or move. We invite you to join us in *Concrete and Ink: Storytelling and the Future of Architecture* over the next hundred and sixty pages.

THE

BELOW

HOUSE

Ben Okri

They lived in a house that was on the street off the main road. There was a marshland in front of the house, where mosquitoes bred. Along the little street, which used to be a dirt track, till it was made more useable by the cars and lorries that drove down it, there were workshops for mechanics. The bodywork of the yellow buses that ply the Lagos streets were built in places like the mechanics' workshops. In the mornings the sparks from their welding equipment could be seen. The mechanics, as they were called, never wore any face gear.

Further on down the street was an abattoir. Next to it was a school. Sometimes the goats that were to be slaughtered were tethered in the school building after class hours. The goats sensed the imminence of their deaths. Perhaps it was the mood of the place, haunted by the ghosts of so many dead animals.

Opposite the school was the house where they lived. It seemed like an old house, but it was not as old as it looked. The house had been built as the second house the landlord owned. The first one was a long bungalow crammed with tenants who had huge families. Sometimes as many as six or seven people lived in one room. The second house was a two-storey building. The mother had taken a two-room flat on the ground floor. There was another family at the back. She didn't see them often. The rooms were small, but she had managed to make the first into a living room and the second into a bedroom. These rooms had to hold all the items of a life that covered two continents. She lived there with her sons.

The house had been built as part of the free-for-all scramble for land that happened as the city expanded westwards. Without original permits as such, with papers often put together after some bribe to the right people in the department of land development, landlords built their houses wherever they found space. There was originally little planning. That came later. Roads grew from paths that were once tracks that led to little hamlets and isolated communities in the bush. The city expanded and encompassed them, and the tracks used by cows and goats became paths and then roads. They had never been tarred and so were hard and dusty in the dry season and turned to mud in the rainy season.

The houses were built somewhat haphazardly. Some were at an angle to the road. Then another would be set in complete contradiction to the others. The angles were all wrong but no one noticed. No one had done a comprehensive survey of the land either, and streets sprang up because someone stuck a name on a plank of wood and that first sign became the street's name. Sometimes streets acquired their names through rumour or through proximity to some factory or notable place in the neighbourhood, which could be a celebrated *buka* or a local market.

When the mother moved into the house, it was a fine-looking building, mustard-coloured, four-square in the bright sunlight. Within a year, its paint had faded, had peeled, and the building was now a mouse-grey colour, the colour of dirt and mud and finger stains. The doors were bright blue, the roof seemed of solid zinc, and it was the main building you saw from the bus stop across the marshland. It had a grey wall round its edges to deter thieves. All the windows had metal grilles with locks so they couldn't be opened from the outside. The wall had barbed wire running along its top, and seen from inside, it looked as if you were not in your house but inside a small-sized prison.

By the second year not only had the brightness of the doors faded and cracked and the toilets become clogged and impossible to use, but the strangest thing of all, which no one noticed for a long time, was that when you came out of the house you found the outside world aslant, somewhat out of kilter. For a long time, they were possessed of the certainty that the world had tilted on its axis, that things had gone wrong, that the land had been twisted from its original orientation. They sensed it every day as they went out, whether it was to work or to school. It was only when they came back into the house that the world made sense again.

The family were kept very close together by the skewing of the world, the broken axis of things. They drew close and told one another stories and reinforced themselves with a mythology of the family that they created every day. That they lived on the edge of desperation meant nothing. That the mother worked hard at maintaining her dignity against the outrages of an undignified world meant absolutely nothing. These things only strengthened their mythology, only deepened the intensity of their closeness.

Outside the house, the world was disintegrating. No one seemed to notice. More houses were built in the mind-boggling disorder of the area. Some people built their houses right into the street. Some built their houses at street corners, forcing those who walked to navigate their way around their houses. Every day foundations were sunk into the ground and metal poles stuck up out of the earth and concrete mixers whirled outside the yard and, before you knew it, a new two-storey building, waiting to be weighed down with families groaning with poverty, sprang up.

The front rooms became beer parlours or carpenters' sheds or barber shops. Neon-lit signboards appeared advertising the new establishment. Sometimes it was a new record shop. *Apala* music or the thumping vibrations of Afrobeat would pound in the air along with the dust that rose with the scooters and the yellow taxis that struggled along the impromptu streets. Meanwhile outside there were coups followed by coups. The daily newspapers coughed up the black phlegm of daily outrages to the public coffers. Vast funds went missing, politicians were accused of kickbacks, military governors awarded themselves vast contracts for roads that would never be built, and children went to school in unfinished school buildings, with half-built walls through which they could see the goats tethered and waiting in horror to be slaughtered.

The mother lived in all of this with great dignity. She held up her family with the salt of proverbs and the magic of stories. She had dreams in which her children, one by one, in their different spheres, would triumph in the world. The bad water and the ruined sewers affected her health and she kept her ailing condition to herself. But to her children she showed not only remarkable courage but also unfailing good humour. She had a story for everything and there was not anything good or bad that she could not transfigure with a story.

But the world was tilting. The world was sinking. The city throbbed with energy and rage. People argued everywhere. The buses belched out clouds of poisonous fumes. The factories darkened the skyline with their dark emissions. Along the streets roadside traders hollered and sometimes chanted their wares. Children returned from school with their faces creased with dirt and smoke, their clothes dirty from passing through the coagulating fumes in the air.

Sometimes in the evenings there were spectacular parties. Whole streets were taken over for weddings or funeral celebrations. Once there was a wedding party that went on for three days. None of the neighbours had been consulted. The streets were laid out with tables and chairs and guests came in lace wrappers and gorgeous, pyramidal head ties, the men in *sokoto* and *agbadas*, the children in the matching outfits of their parents. A band played on an improvised stand and well into the night their voices rang over the houses and the fume-covered banana plants and the dusty palm trees. Always at these parties there were quarrels and fights, tears and curses. The dramatic reconciliations were almost as violent as the altercations that caused them.

No one knew that the world was unstable. The world rested on nothing and they weighed it down with all that passion, all that disorder. The earth was unstable too. No one had consulted her. No one had spoken to her, asked her permission, or investigated her disposition. Everything was laid on her: vast skyscrapers, thundering lorries, gigantic drilling machines. All night the road roared with vehicles. It never stopped. From the house, the road and the world could be heard as through an infinite microphone. When you didn't hear it with your ears, you felt it through the vibration of things.

Then one day the mother stepped out of the house and found that the door was not at the right level. She had to step higher to go out. She had to duck her head acutely so as not to crack it against the upper part of the jamb. On another day one of the sons coming back home from work noticed that he couldn't quite find the house. He had to look harder than before; and with an extraordinary effort of will he brought it back into being, as if pulling it up from oblivion. One of the sons had gone away for a long time and came back and confirmed for himself that all things tend to shrink in memory, and that the world one used to know is always smaller in reality. Everything seemed smaller to him on his return. The school building seemed sadder and smaller, the goats seemed scrawnier, and the bungalow behind their house seemed like an enlarged matchbox. Their house was unrecognisable. It was hotter inside. Fabulous ingenuity was now conscripted in the moving of bowels. There were now so many new houses in the area that the street had become an obstacle course.

The heat made everything worse and tempers flared and policemen took to flogging cars and motorcyclists and in compounds and rooms voices were raised to an unnatural pitch. The economy staggered along and the elections were rigged and every few years the military came back in coups.

The house that they lived in grew unbearably hot at night and not even the ceiling fan made sleep easier. The mother grew thinner, worked harder, helped her relations, and one by one her children flew the nest. On the day the eldest left she was driving him to the airport when he looked back at the house with tears of fondness. It was the house in which he had been nourished with his mother's love and with stories. He had been close to his brothers. The rooms were small but the stories they shared made them vast. Sometimes they would tell one another stories till late into the night. They told stories while the family upstairs quarrelled so hard that they added to the weight of the house. They told stories through coups and the return to democracy, through the sapping of the nation's resources and through the constant failures of electricity. He stood there and looked at the house as if for the first time and it was then he noticed something that had evaded him all along. But what he noticed could not be true. It must have been an illusion produced by the strong emotion of leaving.

He noticed that the house was smaller but also that it seemed to be disappearing into the earth. The top floor was much lower than it had been years ago. He looked and blinked and was about to share this discovery with his mother, but she looked at her watch and reminded him of the length of the journey to the airport and of the terrible traffic they had to deal with. They set off immediately and he forgot all about the strange condition of the house. He travelled to France and Greece and to the United States of America. Then he settled in England where he devoted himself to the study of meaning.

The house kept quiet about its condition. This was not always the case. Sometimes the house spoke but no one listened. The landlord, increasingly certain that the house was in one of the prime locations of the city, doubled his rent. For the first time the mother began to think of leaving. The house spoke to the tenants but they were too terrified to hear. The house spoke to the landlord but he was too proud and greedy to think that the house even had a right to speak for itself. So the house sank into its own silence and communed with the earth.

One day a daughter of the tenant that lived in the back rooms tried to leave the house to go to school, but found that she could not leave. The door would not open. Her parents thought she was looking for an excuse not to go to school and with a great effort they got the door open. They could not understand what had happened. That night the mother had a dream that the house was becoming a tomb and that she was living not in a house but in a pharaonic coffin. She had been reading a book about ancient Egypt which spoke of the coffins not as places of death, but the beginnings of the house of eternity. The dream had so troubled the mother that she decided that the time really had come for her to leave. A month later she and her remaining children hired a lorry. They had great trouble bringing out her bed and her tables and sofas because the door had somehow become too small for them. At last everything was out and they were set to leave. The mother took one last look at the house, just as her eldest son had done some time ago, and what she saw amazed her. The house now seemed to only be the hat that was the top floor with a tiny bit of the lower walls visible. It did not seem possible to her that she had been living in a house that had been vanishing all this time. How is it that none of them had seen it? Was it the tyranny of daily perception, or had the house somehow conspired to envelop them in its fantasy? The mother was about to say something of what she saw to her sons, but the driver of the lorry had a bout of that inescapable Lagosian impatience and wanted to be off so he could get in a few more jobs for the day. So the mother said nothing and, as they drove off, she retained in her mind the image of the shrunken house that had been her home.

The mother moved onto her own land and a house she built and no longer thought about the house she had left behind. But the house thought of her. The house missed her stories. She had thought she was telling stories to her children and receiving their stories in turn, but they had all been sharing their stories with the house. That was why the house had managed to delay its disappearance into the earth. All those stories kept it buoyant, made it float, as it were, to the rhythms of other lands, other homes, other destinies.

When the mother left, the landlord rented her rooms to a large family of ten. They brought with them squabbles and noise. They had to crawl in through the top of the front door, which had been removed altogether, and when they went out for the day, they had to crawl out. They brought the weight of their troubles and their hunger. The young children cried all night in the loathsome unrelieved heat.

Then came the politicians. They were seasoned in the art of taking without giving and they cared not very much for the earth or the fumes or the lungs of the inhabitants or the loss of the forests or the terror of the goats or the unfinished school building where the students carried on their incomplete education.

And the house, starved of stories, deprived of fine and far-fetched dreams, lost its levity and its humour.

Then one day, just before the big rains that swept in from the east, the house lost the will to go on existing, lost the will to maintain its coherence. But the tenants went on living there, for years and years to come. They went on living there even when the house had sunk completely into the earth, so completely that only the top storey roof was now visible.

The landlord had provided ladders and ropes for the tenants who lived now below the earth to emerge when they went to work or school. He was even kind enough to provide them with light extensions and free candles when the electricity failed, hour after hour, all through the nights and through most of the day. The family lived below the earth like human rats. Out of their window they saw only the earth. Sometimes water from below seeped up into the living room. The landlord showed his understanding by lowering the rent for the duration of the seepage. The family of ten lived down there huddled and enclosed all around by the dark and the heat. Sometimes in their silence, in the blaze of their eyes staring with anxiety at one another, they heard scattered fragments of all the stories that the house had stored and played back to itself in the twilight of its existence.

Then one day the house disappeared and no one knew that it had ever been there.

CITY

Sophie Mackintosh

My supervisor called me in for a meeting to brief me the day before we were due to go to the wild city. She was going to come with me, having been on trips there before, but not for some time. *I just want you to understand what we are dealing with*, she said. She seemed a little off, her fingernails picking at the laminated cover of her notebook where it was peeling. It was late afternoon, when the smog peaked, and the heat made it worse. The sweaty collar of my shirt rubbed at my throat.

Of course, I told her. I had specialised in this city after all, researched it and read and gorged myself on every case study. Ever since childhood it had held a deep fascination for me. I would crawl underneath my bed in the room I shared with my sister with a magazine I'd found somewhere, documenting streets where the foliage burst through cracks and bears walked up what had once been main roads. Back then we lived in one of the usual blocks at the edge of another city, a long way away but the same as every other city, with the windows sealed shut. In the night we slipped on our air purifiers, pink plastic guards over our face, filtering any still night air that might have got in. My mother and I nurtured plants in our flat which covered every free surface, almost every shelf, crowding the floor of our bedrooms. We made our own ecosystem.

My supervisor and I went in on foot. Cars had been one of the first things to go, the first thing the city banned. There was no hard border, but a thick ring of forest to delineate in and out. Before reaching these trees, there was a long swathe of earth, sparsely grassed; not quite wasteland, but nobody lived there either. The trees suggested the relative youth of the city, the oldest planted just thirty years ago. There was a flat low building at the entrance of the forest. Our things were searched, which I had expected, and we were patted down, which I had not. Two cereal bars and a packet of chewing gum, a tissue, were dropped into a plastic bowl and confiscated, as were the cigarettes of my supervisor, which she had hidden in her bra. She smiled winningly at the security guards, threw her hands up and said *You can't fault me for trying, right?* They smiled, but said nothing, they must have been used to it. We showered and changed into more suitable clothes: army-issue greens and browns to blend in, thick boots broken in by someone else.

Beyond the ring of trees, the tower blocks like the one I had grown up in gave the first clue to the new rules we were in, aside from the lack of cars. Greenery flourished from the broken windows, vines curling all the way down the sides. Long grass and smaller trees grew at the base. *Nobody lives here any more*, the supervisor told me. I was transported back to childhood, as if the plants we had nurtured had sprung out and down, dripping along the sides.

If *home* was not just a physical thing but a feeling, it was there in the wild city I first felt it. There it pulsed through me for the first time. It wasn't to do with aesthetics, or with function, but with fit. It was untranslatable. It was like the word I'd heard once, somewhere – *hiraeth* – which had no counterpart in English but meant a nostalgic longing for elsewhere. I had been waiting for this feeling in the rooms of houses all my life, standing on floors of concrete or varnished wood or carpet, and in the blueprints of the houses I designed, leafing through them, visualising how they would stand against the earth. I waited for it walking around the city with the sleek filter of my mask hissing my own breath back to me, reassuringly, cutting the sound of the traffic as well as the fumes, and yet it never really found me, or the feeling that had found me was a paltry relative of this one, which was all certainty and light. But could you trust a feeling like this? It wasn't quantifiable, and I dealt in quantities and figures – in air quality and units of value, in a push-pull between flimsiness and strength, longevity and cost. Perhaps to trust in a feeling like that was what my supervisor had been warning me against at the start. A sentimentality that was engrained in us, this desire to return to the natural and to communing with it, which was risky, because romanticism often just got in the way.

Jennifer was the mayor, though the word 'mayor' didn't seem quite right. She didn't wear a suit or a big medallion around her neck. She wore the clothes of everyone else in the city – the last of the foraged fibres, unpicked and refashioned, tanned hides from animals caught in traps. In our camouflage gear we felt quite overdressed. I asked her when I got to know her better why they didn't wear the clothes we did, and she told me that being in the city was a process of feeling as much as learning, and that once you looked at their lifestyle as something beyond a habit, you would realise that it was something that connected everything around them – rather than seeing where sustainability began and ended, you would see it didn't end at all. *Okay,* I said, *but isn't it hard to let go of comfort?* And she said that they hadn't. *Was it comfortable for you, to fill your lungs with smog?* she asked me, and I thought again about that flat filled with green, the masks we wore at night.

I had dreamed wearing those masks, dreams I thought inspired by the magazines I read before sleep. *New Kind of City. Future City Gives Hope.* Foliage on the covers, and ruins. In the dreams I walked over roads of cracking tarmac with ferns uncurling through the fissures. Rabbits darted ahead of me; birds overhead, starlings, forming a cloud. There was the faint smell of fire in the air, the sound of voices from the houses I passed. I was going somewhere, there was purpose in my step.

I walked like that through the wild city in the first days. A mantra in my head: *the dreams brought me here, the dreams call me back.* The sky was navy and pink. Already the thought of leaving made me feel panicked. There was a darkening resentment too. *Why show me this and then take it away?* I was in what felt like pre-emptive mourning, and it was confusing to me, because I had just arrived, and I knew I was only here temporarily, to learn and then to go back. My task was to return to my own city and display my findings, suggestions we could incorporate, which I already knew would be discarded, because the wild city, for most of us, was only something to make us feel better, something academic that had been done for the sake of doing – an example for a new way of being that would never take root, not with us, because we were too used to the way things were, because somewhere we liked the smog, found it comforting, and it was too large to think about breaking away.

In a city where nothing could be built, or not in the way that I understood it, a new kind of symbiosis had to be found. But it wasn't one that came naturally, Jennifer told me, as she showed me from house to house, and the communal areas for sorting foraged things, butchery, the making of necessary things. I found myself taking more care with every step, seeing things like the yellow heart of a flower I'd never seen before, or an emphatic star in the dirt. It was natural to want to repair, to replace a fallen brick or pane of glass, she explained. There had to be a mindset shift, from fear to acceptance. They treated the crumbling houses as normal, but carefully, anxious not to trigger rot, to try and keep them intact for as long as possible. Beyond that, when they started to fall beyond repair, they adapted. The realisation that things could leave little trace, that a roof could be mud or thatch or pleated branches, that a house could slowly leave its houseness behind and return to *shelter*, return to *home*, to the point when things fell, was almost a celebration for what could spring up in its stead. And the knowledge that when these things of hay bales and leaves fell too, as they would, the earth would enfold them back so easily.

I first felt it – this *home* – in the house where we would be staying. *Drop your bags*, the expedition leader told us. It had once been a small apartment complex, two storeys high. Enough remained of it that I could recognise – a bathtub in the former bathroom now used as a planter for tomatoes and herbs, a little patch of tiling in a corner kept, perhaps, for decorative reasons. I ran my hand over a portion of remaining original wall, the useless light-switch still there, the layers of plasterboard and brick and a curl of dirty white paint still visible, and one unbroken window, the rotten sill overgrown with yellow-blooming woad. Apart from this, the roof was latticed branches, a waterproofed layer of the same woad. It smelled fresh and green. The tall glass door leading out onto what must have once been a patio was long-shattered, but fragments like jewels remained in the grass. I found them when I went on my hands and knees to take samples of the earth, but also to remember what soil could feel like, its wet smell, and what could be lurking inside it – the teeming ants and the snails with their shells. Sometimes in the other city, back again in my childhood, the mirror city in another world from here, a prize was a skinny earthworm pulled from yellowed grass. Anaemic, too-dry. *Put them back*, I told the other children, not out of fear of the worm but rather fear for it.

My supervisor didn't have the fascination I did. She took notes too, sure, samples and recordings. We spoke to many people who'd lived in the city for varying amounts of time, some since the start, some only a few years. They stopped accepting applications for new dwellers (that was what they called themselves, dweller, a name lovelier and closer to the ground), because there were too many people who wanted to come, and they had to expand slowly, mindful of every additional person's impact. *When we are dead and gone*, the dwellers said into my recorder – all of them seemed to hold this idea at the forefront of what they did – *we want to be peaceful knowing that no trace will be left. That the only traces came not from us, but from before, and even those will have sunk back into the earth.*

It makes me feel strange, my supervisor said at the end of each day, as we sorted our notes before the sun went down and we joined a little fire or made our own, before sleeping early. I could agree with her that there were moments of uncanniness in seeing former shopping centres overgrown and ransacked, deer skittering around fountains, in how abandoned cars were just skeletons in the grass. But I saw beauty in it too, where she didn't. *Everything leaves something on the earth*, she said, as we stamped on the embers and wrapped ourself in our sleeping bags, the dark creeping in. *This city and our own are just two sides of the same coin. We can no more erase ourselves than fix what we made. We just have to do the best we can.* She looked at me. *Don't forget that you're only here so you can come back*, she said. *Don't let it get a grip on you. It's not what you think.*

Perhaps we used to take nature for granted, when we could walk wherever, pick flowers and eat blackberries carelessly, push beaches away from our faces. I had such a love for everything I was seeing around me, it felt almost wrong – powerful, shameful even, like crying after a long time of emotional peace. I went for quick walks alone before my supervisor woke up, eager to drink in as much as I could, and I breathed consciously, deeply, as if I could scour my lungs of their damage.

    Live lightly, I wrote in my notebook, like we didn't already know it. *Use what's already used*, I wrote, like we didn't already know this either. We knew it all. There would just be no implementing. It was simple, it was laid out for us. I was getting angrier throughout the day as I trailed around, watched children playing and everyone living their peaceful life. I wanted this life to be mine, I wanted it, even when it rained and the mud dripped from the roofs. In my own city we wore sturdy hoods to protect against the caustic rain, but here it was safe, tentatively, and I let it drip down the back of my neck, making my whole body uncomfortable, and it was wonderful.

I slept less and less. I dreamed the same dreams I had dreamed all those years ago, maskless now, and wasn't afraid of how exactly they corresponded. I spent more time with Jennifer and her family, serene in the greenish light of their home. We ate dandelion leaves and drank elderflower cordial and spoke about beauty. My supervisor started talking to me about wrapping up the project early. She stared at me hard whenever I was around her. *There's a lot more we need to do here*, I told her, and she shook her head. Jennifer told me to move into their house, so we could speed up the things I was learning, and though my supervisor shouted at me, I remained impassive.

Stay, Jennifer said to me on the first night in her home. All the children were singing. In the morning I went back to what had been the base camp, and the supervisor had gone. My notes and research too, except for my diary which I kept hidden on my body. *You're here now*, they said to me when I returned, and everybody hugged me, and it felt right.

The thing about a body is that a body can be a home and a home can be a body; soft crook of the elbow, long curve of the neck. My skin was mapped with veins, leaflike. Inside, my body carried the things it accumulated. Still held the dark smog, tarred against the alveoli. Each bad thing breathed and eaten becomes a cell, the root of a hair, a tooth or rib.

I was given my own room, to risk no contamination to the others. I was prescribed baths of salt and water and clay, in which I dipped my body and emerged, monstrous, coated in the mixture. Breathing exercises. I sat closest to the fire to breathe in the hot air, to dissolve the impurities filling me like silt. Even those plants in the flat where I had grown up hadn't sluiced me in enough oxygen, could never do enough. Jennifer was apologetic. *Sorry, so sorry*, she told me. *But this will be worth it, I promise.*

Periods of prescribed fasting; borage leaf tea and tansy and the dew sucked from grass. Soon there was no need to eat at all. I could only be remade with what was around me. When my skin started to come off, we bound it with spiderwebs. When my bones started to fail it was no problem to use twigs, green wood for the pliable joints.

Sorry, we're sorry, she said, but I didn't mind. Little white pebbles for my teeth. Butterfly wings for my eyelids. Every change brought me closer.

I know now what the dreams meant. I walk through the city like I never was elsewhere, like there never were floors of polished concrete, of paving stone and carpet and floorboard. Moonlight and daylight are the same to me. I crawl through the undergrowth and am met by creatures, scurrying insects. Above me, the old towers in the sky are full of bird nests, fruiting shrubs, some staircases still standing. In the rooms there are old televisions with broken screens, unholstered chairs dissolving into dust. I flex my new knuckles. I breathe deep with my clean, expansive lungs.

RED

STORIES

ROAD

Alison Irvine

Finlay's Story

See that flat? I am born there. 1968. Count twenty-five windows from the ground and you will find me and my big brother, my mum and dad, an inside toilet, electric heaters and a veranda. The rent is higher than our room and kitchen in Bridgeton. But my dad works and our neighbours work and people are pleased to be here so it is the best of places to live. We live in one of the gleaming towers in the sky. They knock my block down in 2012 but we won't get as far as that.

A girl lives in one of the low-down houses and imagines the Red Road flats are hotels. She thinks we have lots of friends. We do. See those children? I am one of those boys. We're out from nine in the morning till ten at night; fifty, sixty, seventy, eighty, a hundred kids playing on four fields and a football pitch. We play tennis and squash against the gable ends, we head footballs thrown from windows and call it Giant Headers, we play Olympics, we play boxing, we make football goalposts from beer kegs or jumpers. I hear the click click click of players' boots on concrete after a long game. We pass girls playing elastics or peever.

See? I have a good childhood. No sectarianism: I don't care who I play with even if some of my mates go to All Saints and I go to The Albert. I have friends in all the blocks. We ride to the hills on bikes and boys will take birds' eggs and one boy takes a kestrel and keeps it on his veranda and we follow him to the field to watch him work it. Just like in the film.

See my mum on her veranda? She spots me on the field and knows I am safe. See other mothers? They think we're too far away. They don't like it. They wish for a low-down house with a front and back door.

The lifts are soon trouble. Only two in our massive slab block. That's my mum stuck all night. That's me stuck and the firemen coming to rescue me, pulling me through the hatch at the top. Bikes, prams, shopping bags – there's little room for all of us. Undertakers can't keep a coffin flat so they lean it upright against a lift wall. When a lift breaks down, there are no stairs off the landing to climb down to the ground, so that's me, knocking on somebody's door asking to be let through their flat to use the back stairs. Drug addicts will later drag the bodies of dead friends to these back stairs.

But for now the landings are sparkling. My mum checks the rota and takes her turn. Kind neighbours set the lift doors to open at the pensioners' floors and have just enough time to run out to deliver their papers and run in before the doors close. Sometimes they step on mats laid across the landing to stop footprints muddying the freshly cleaned floors. I play soldiers on the landing. I play Subbuteo and boxing and if we get chased for being too noisy, we gather in the sheds next to the flats' foyers. Here, we keep away from the weather. Here, girls set out jumble sale stalls on weekends. Here, we witness the death of a man who throws himself from a window – denims, rucksack, green khaki army jacket.

In bad weather our bathwater sloshes and our lightshades swing. Built to accommodate the wind, the building sways. But wind still gusts around the bases of the blocks. It lifts me off my feet and throws me onto the concrete when I am coming home from primary school.

In time we are chased by glue sniffers from Avonspark Street. Kids from gangs across the railway line charge at us with stones and sticks when we are playing football and we have to run away or chase them back. Glue sniffers start to walk on the girders at the top of the blocks and because of them, and because of the jumpers, the doors are closed and my mum can no longer hang her sheets on the high washing lines. We navigate violence and gangs like that Didier Pasquette who attempts to cross the high wire between two single blocks, many years after I am gone.

Mobile shops come to the flats. After seven years there is a paved court with shops: baker, shoe shop, newsagent, butcher, mini supermarket, gift shop and more. There are buses to bigger shops in Springburn and buses into the town too. They'll say we have no amenities, they'll say we have no transport, but we do. And see even below the concrete? There's a bingo hall, a bookies and a pub. So while the women go to the bingo, the men drink next door at the Brig Bar or bet. And buses and buses of women will come to the bingo and when buses and buses of refugees from Kosovo come, long after me, families will donate clothes and toys to the first of Red Road's asylum seekers.

See our lumber room, it has no windows. My brother and I take turns to sleep in here beneath my mum's hanging washing. We drill through the wall to run an extension lead from the living room to our record player. We don't tell the housing because there's asbestos in the walls. I don't care because I play my Bowie records and The Police records, and when I am a teenager with a hangover, I will be glad of the dark, windowless room. Aged nine, however, with dreams of becoming a fireman, Ten Red Road Court catches fire and fire engines come. I see nothing and hear nothing and I am sad to miss the excitement. Although there's a tragedy. And after the fire some tenants refuse to return and they move out to new housing schemes in Cumbernauld. It's only 1977. Red Road's gleam is tarnishing.

See the asbestos: the council can't replace a window for fear of dislodging it. When I'm twelve, men in white protective suits work on our flat to attempt to make it safe. The council can do little to maintain the blocks because of the asbestos. They build additional staircases on our slab blocks so we don't have to walk through people's houses when the lifts break down. They build walls between the blocks, separating one from the other. Whereas once we ran through the whole scheme effortlessly, now we are guided along concrete-walled paths. Those walls will get you mugged. Too many alleys and dead spots.

But concierges come to replace the caretakers. Day shifts, back shifts and night shifts. CCTV and door entry systems. You're less likely to be stuck in a lift all night. The concierges know every face and do favours for the elderly. They talk to police and phone noisy flats. And most neighbours don't mind a little noise. They like a party and cling to community spirit. Until housebreakers move in. Or flats are left empty and used as giro drops. Or people fling mattresses or furniture or nappies from their verandas. Or heroin takes a hold of some of our kids. The boy I box with, we lose him to heroin. People lose their jobs or move in when they've got no job and have problems which make it hard for them to look after themselves, let alone the buildings. No more mats to protect the landing floors. The eighties is a cruel decade. We lose my dad after an illness and my mum, who trains as a nurse, no longer likes high-rise living. She never grows to like the lifts. Red Road isn't the same any more. Old neighbours, the good neighbours, move out. My best friend moves away to stay out of trouble. There's more to come. But you know how it ends. Years after me, a kestrel will nest on the roof of one of the blocks and will delay the demolition. And I will lament the loss of Red Road.

I leave when I'm twenty-three. I'm a fireman and have children who think my childhood is poor. Yet despite their phones and online lives, they say they might like a block full of kids to play with. I have good memories. Perhaps I catch Red Road at the right time. We are young together and, for me, I am cared for and nurtured as I grow.

But I am not born yet. My parents are still waiting for their room and kitchen to be inspected by the Corporation. If it's acceptable, they'll be given a flat at Red Road. Families are still sleeping four and five to a bed and sharing a toilet on the landing. The Corporation is overspending but it is worth it. We're one of hundreds of families waiting to move into our gleaming tower in the sky, to create great lives out of all that steel and concrete and hope.

Fragment of transcript
of interview with Finlay McKay

When we grew up there was one, two, three, four big fields and a football field where you could play. We would go out from nine o'clock in the morning to ten o'clock at night. We'd play whatever was in: Olympics, tennis. Non stop. You'd always have about fifty, sixty, seventy, eighty, a hundred kids all out playing on different fields. Sometimes you couldn't get on the field because of the games of football going on. You'd have one game going one way and another game the other way.

We painted the tennis courts during the night. Before they started building all these walls and stuff there was a wee wall and it was perfect for a tennis court. Me and my pal painted them for a laugh. Two of the blocks had tennis courts built in them. So one night, me and my pal, we would have been about twelve or something, we got hold of a pot of paint and a brush and we thought how are we going to get straight lines? Somehow, I don't know how, we acquired a door, a front door, and all dressed in black, two or three in the morning, we came down and painted it.

Needful Things

Mbali lived in Red Road, on the twenty-sixth floor of one of the towers. She and her husband had come from Zimbabwe in 2001, with employment visas and their two daughters, and they stayed in Red Road for five years. I've changed her name at her request, for personal reasons that will become clear, but everything else in this story is as truthful as her memory allows. I've interviewed Mbali twice, formally, and we've exchanged a handful of emails over the ten years we've known each other. We chatted most recently just as the Covid-19 lockdown was easing in the summer of 2020. 'Mention the tennis rackets,' she said to me after our last conversation and I promised I would.

At first, she was in awe of Red Road's two vast slab blocks and six towers that the architects called point blocks. 'We don't have tower blocks in Zimbabwe, all houses are bungalows. We were so high up. I loved the view. There was lots of sky and I could see everyone around me, and I could see the places I had been and where I wanted to go to.' In the distance she saw what could have been a golf course: 'I'm not sure but it was lovely. So nice. And I feel like, oh my goodness, you can walk around with fresh air and maybe run around.' She saw the Tesco and the Lidl too, closer to the flats, and watched the buses travelling to and from the city.

Mbali asked for a furnished flat and paid a hundred pounds a month extra for furniture which soon, because it was old and unattractive, she piled into a box room with no windows and kept behind a closed door. They bought new furniture. The flat was large. The living room was big enough for a dining area with a table and a lounge area with a sofa and a television. They put 'Scotland's Towns' pictures on the living room walls alongside photographs of family, and they bought Scottish-themed tea towels too. Mbali liked the homeware shop in Red Road's parade which sold candles, light bulbs, wooden spoons, trays and mats for teapots. She couldn't remember the shop's name and said perhaps it was called: You Might Like This. I asked a friend, Finlay, born and brought up in Red Road, if he knew of its name. He told me he remembered the shop being called Needful Things. He said the owners changed the name every six months or so, and it probably wasn't called Needful Things, in homage to the Stephen King novel, for long.

Red Road was quiet on the twenty-sixth floor. Mbali and her family shared a landing with an elderly woman and a very young couple with a baby. When the wind blew, the building swayed. Her husband filled the bath tub and gathered the family round to watch the water slosh from side to side. The toilet water did the same.

One fresh and windy day, soon after they moved to Red Road, Mbali saw some tennis rackets in a shop and bought them, hoping that her daughters would play. She couldn't find a court. 'Houses all around and nowhere to go,' she told me. 'No playgrounds.' She wished there had been a sign in her tower block's foyer: 'If they had told us about football or tennis, where to go, we would have gone there. We didn't know about the community.'

Mbali worked as a supply teacher, her husband as an electrical engineer. The girls went to local schools. She made a friend, a Somali woman, who took her to the African shops on Great Western Road and Allison Street. She made more friends. They cooked meat on a *braai* (a barbecue) on their veranda. They danced to Brenda Fassie's party songs. Mbali's voice was high and energetic when she told me about the friends she made and the fun she had. It took on a low tone when she slowed to tell me of their troubles.

Mbali considered going to Essex to live with her sister to train to be a nurse, but she didn't want to leave her daughters in Red Road with the children who knocked on the door and kept her girls out late. She thought her husband might struggle to look after them. He had begun to drink. He had started to come home after bedtime, turning on the lights and waking the family with his noise.

Their young neighbours knocked on the door. 'They would come at night and ask for milk. "Oh the baby has no milk." And usually we'd give it to them. But it went on and on and they were always asking asking asking.' The man had come to the door to sell radios too, just when Mbali and her family moved in. The radio he tried to sell them was dearer than in Tesco. Mbali declined.

Their flat was burgled. Her daughter's phone was taken. Mbali's husband slept while it happened. He woke and came eye to eye with the burglar. As Mbali's husband called out and stood up in his half-sleep, the thief ran away. Then the young neighbours left. 'We just saw the big door put by the council. A metal door. And when they took out that couple, they didn't open the door again.' The quiet lady who lived on the landing moved out too. 'And then it was deserted. The other houses were empty: one, two, three, four. So lonely. Very scary on the landing. Unless we could hear someone walking around, the concierge, it was very quiet.'

Her daughters looked out of their windows and asked why they couldn't live in one of the houses they saw at the foot of the flats. 'They would say "Why are we living up here? This is a poor place. We're surrounded by houses. Why can't we stay in these houses?"' Mbali thought the houses were for white people only. 'Black people lived in the tall buildings,' she told herself. At the same time as tenants from other blocks were being decanted by Glasgow Housing Association into homes in the surrounding areas of Balornock and Barmulloch, one point block remained full. This tower, managed by the YMCA, housed asylum seekers. Mbali's daughters called Red Road a *mhaji* place. 'A place for people who are coming from outside the country. People who are still new to the town. Like wearing – what is the name of those shoes you wear – rubber? Flip flops. People wear them in Africa. New people in Red Road wore them.'

Mbali continued to work as a teacher on supply. She couldn't get a permanent job. Their flat in Red Road was cold and damp with mould on the walls. They spent at least twenty pounds a week on their pay-as-you-go electricity meter. 'It wasn't double glazed. You could feel the chilly air coming in. We covered the window with a blanket. I was afraid my daughter would have an asthma attack.' Mbali put her family's name on a housing association's waiting list. They waited for months. Her daughters wanted trainers. Her husband spent more and more of his wages on alcohol. He continued to come home late and switch on the lights. Her youngest daughter felt different to her classmates. Mbali told me of their conversations.

'Mum, do you know I'm poor at this school? They're wearing this and that.'

'Work for it,' Mbali said.

'How?'

'Books. Books. Go down into your books and pick up prizes. Do good and the teacher will love you. I am a teacher. I know. You don't have trainers but go up the stairs in whatever shoes you are wearing. When your teacher gives you food, which is books, eat it.'

'She did,' Mbali told me. And so did Mbali. She applied to retrain as a teacher at university but wasn't accepted onto the course because she was qualified already. Instead, she studied Health and Safety at the University of the West of Scotland and got a first class degree. But first, she left Red Road.

A man from the housing association came to visit. 'They were looking at those in poor housing to see whose flat was the worst,' Mbali said. Four families' houses were inspected for a chance at one tenement flat. Mbali and her family got that flat. Mbali doesn't know what happened to the other families. 'They were Scottish women,' she said.

In 2006 they moved to Royston and stayed for more than ten years. Royston is where her girls grew up. Royston is where her husband's heavy drinking became too much. He didn't stop, even with his diabetes. He turned on the lights and woke the family night after night. Mbali feared he would leave the stove on. She got little sleep. Eventually: 'Please don't come!' Mbali and her daughters said. 'We want to sleep.'

Her supply teaching work ran out. 'Things were not balancing in the house. No food on the table.' She got work as a carer in a home in Cardonald on the other side of the city. 'I became a no-one person. I didn't belong anywhere. Lots of travelling. Taking two buses.'

Mbali spoke to a doctor and a colleague and a social worker and a mortgage adviser. The doctor said, 'We two sitting here do not have the problem.' Mbali knew her husband didn't want help. Her colleague told her that she too had an alcoholic husband whom she had recently left. The social worker said she had concerns about Mbali's younger daughter, in her last years at school. Her father's alcoholism was affecting her. 'For this child, it became a disaster,' Mbali said. 'Move out,' the social worker said. The mortgage adviser told Mbali she could afford to do it.

In 2019 Mbali moved into a house in Barrhead (a bought house as they say in Glasgow). To her husband she said, 'Come back when you are better.' To me in our interview she said, 'We are having a separation. As long as he changes his behaviour, he's welcome to live with us. But at the moment he believes his choice is good.'

Barrhead is miles from Red Road. There are new houses and older houses, bus links and a train station. There is wide open space and there are frogs in the gardens. Close by, there is a sports club with tennis courts. Soon after they'd moved, taking in all of Barrhead's green, Mbali's younger daughter, a young adult by then, said, 'Mum, this is what I needed.'

'I think about my husband,' Mbali said. 'Maybe that housing contributed to his downfall. If we had lived here in Barrhead, if we'd had this when we came in. It's an open space. Not in those buildings with neighbours not working. It was a poor place. It was not inspiring.' I asked her about the legacy of Red Road. If she were in charge, would she build Red Road again? 'I would not build Red Road in my life!' she said.

During lockdown, having returned to supply teaching, Mbali taught the children of keyworkers in an East-end primary school. In those uneasy months, she and her daughters lived in the new bought house and watched the news, obsessed by the Covid-19 statistics, worried for Mbali's sister in Essex, an agency nurse, perplexed by the numbers of black people dying, coming up with theories and hypotheses. They knocked out a fireplace. The DIY was a distraction from the anguish. Her neighbours saw them lifting out the smashed fireplace pieces one day – 'So that's what you've been doing in lockdown!' – and they laughed together. 'The community is nice,' Mbali said to me.

It is now August 2020. At the end of the summer, Mbali will cross the city again to teach in the school in the shadow of Red Road, a metaphorical shadow because the flats are long gone, demolished between 2012 and 2015. At the end of her furlough, her elder daughter will return to work for British Airways. Her younger daughter will resume her medical degree at the University of Aberdeen. 'The children have done so well,' she said.

I thanked Mbali for our interview and agreed with her about her daughters. That's when she asked me to mention the tennis rackets, bought for her children when the family moved to Red Road, but unused for lack of a court, Barmulloch and Balornock being so unlike Barrhead. She didn't know that, decades before them, Finlay and teams of children had whacked balls against the flats' gable ends and painted makeshift tennis courts within the grounds of Red Road. Those were different days in Red Road's history. Different circumstances for Red Road's tenants. I promised Mbali I would mention the rackets.

**Fragment of transcript of interview
with Mbali**

*My husband was an engineer. He'd fill up the tub with water, right
to the top. And there was so much wind blowing around. We would
watch the water leaning all over.*

(...)

*The view was beautiful at night. Different colours coming up. Straight
lines. Different shades from very bright, all yellow. Quiet? Yes. Inside
the building it was very quiet but go into the lifts and down, you
know you're going to meet much noise.*

(...)

*I wish they can be a place of interest where we can go and look at
them. And all the memories coming back. Because if those flats are
coming down and I have lived there for so long, for five years, I feel
like all my memories are just washed out.*

Red Road Stories is dedicated
to Finlay McKay and Mbali,
former residents of the Red Road flats.

THE TOWER

Matthew Dooley

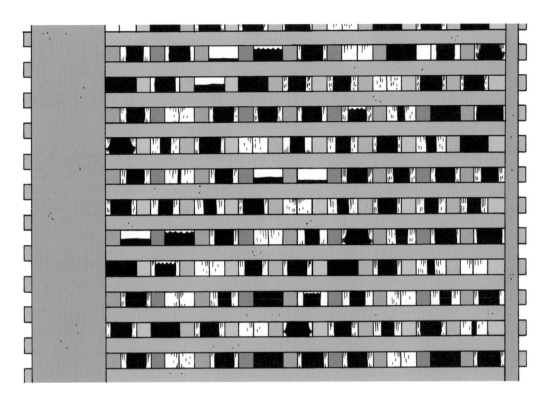

THE TOWER

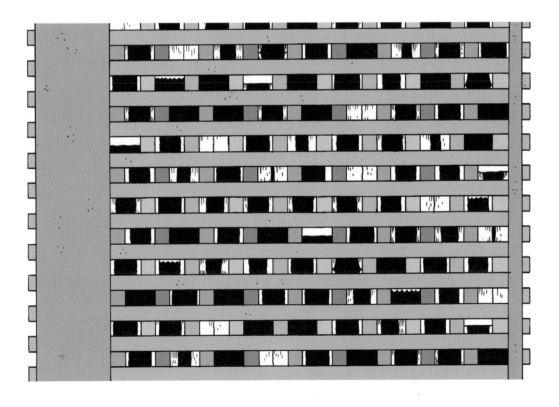

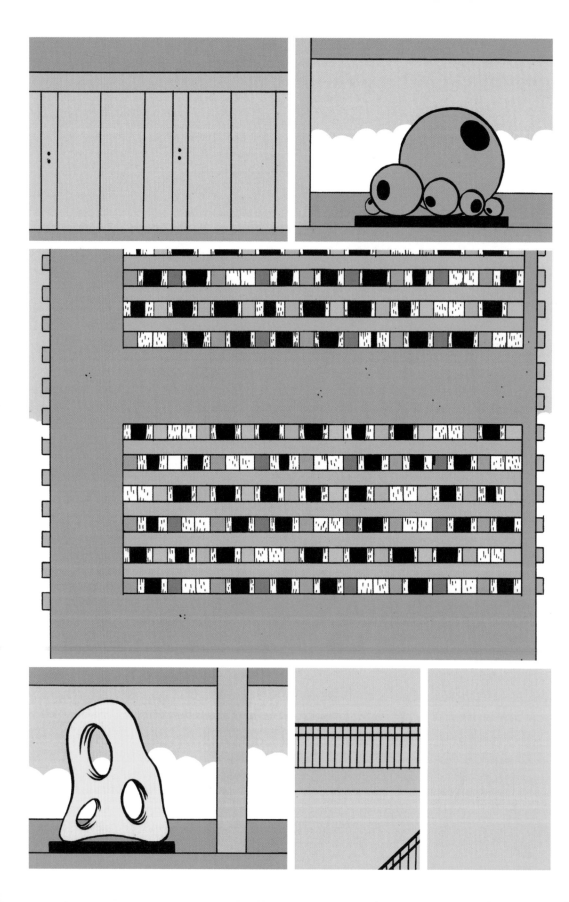

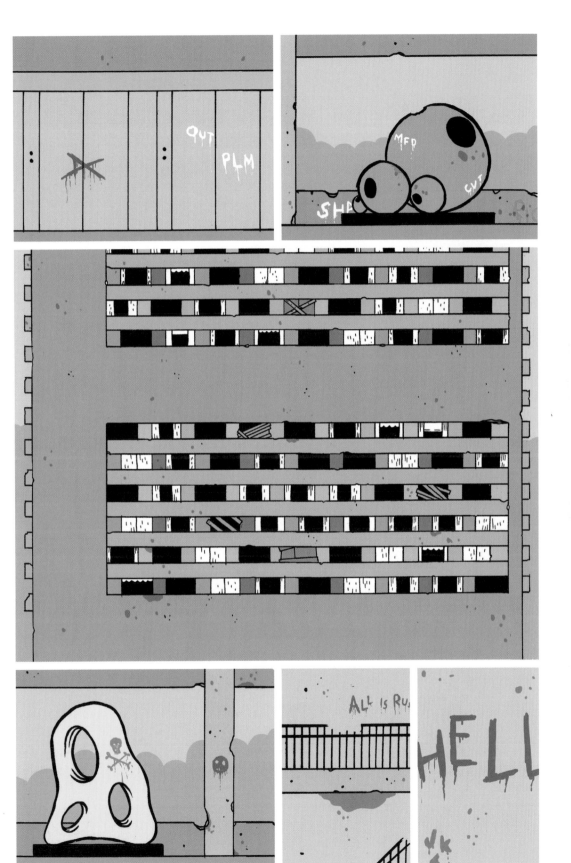

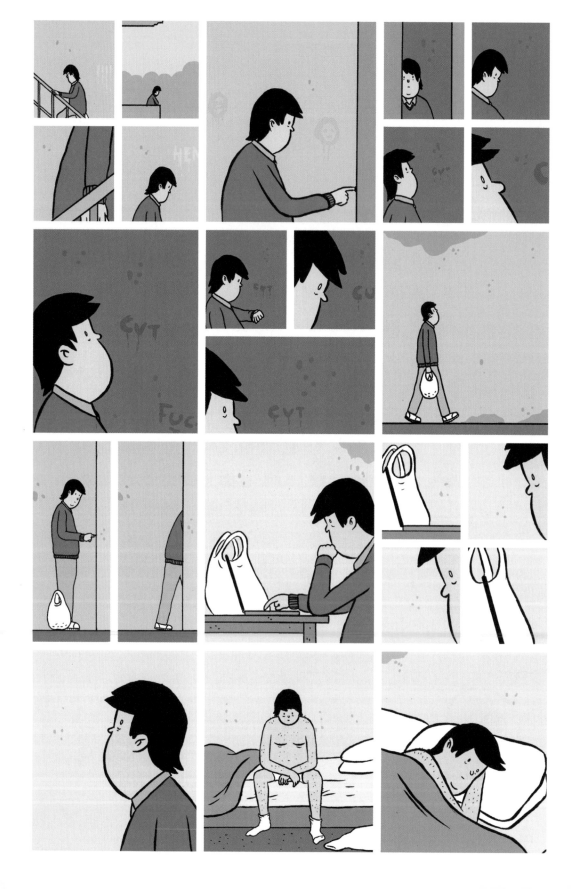

THE

LIFE

AND

HTAED

AND

LIFE

OF ANTIPOLIS

Nina Leger

translated from French by Natasha Lehrer

There was nothing, there would be everything. That was their story.

There was nothing: a hinterland, wild and unpeopled, untamed nature,
        quickened only by the birth and death of plants, the wheeling of birds
        overhead, the song of the cicadas, the passage of the seasons.
There was nothing but the forest,
nothing but streams flowing into one another, furiously roiling the stones
        on the riverbed in the winter, drying up in the summer,
nothing but oak trees rising from the valley floor, pines growing up the
        slopes, pungent odours, white rocky peaks from the tops of which
        you could see the sea, gathered like a pearl in the crook of the
        horizon,
there was nothing,
until a man came
and deposited the developer's kiss upon these lands, to bring them into
        human time,
the time of beginnings that lead to endings, of foundations and what fol-
        lows, of time that's not enough, time that becomes the enemy, time
        that's money, the time of objectives, impatience, anxiety, time that's
        too short, time that can't wait but is in store for us, furtive glances
        at clocks and calendars, the time of promises and commitments,
there was nothing,
until a man
decided:
there would be a city.
And in this city, there would be businesses, laboratories, research insti-
        tutes, universities,
workers, entrepreneurs, decision makers, decision takers, all of whose
        mission would be the invention of the future.
Yes. The purpose of this city would be to give shape to the future.
Of course there would be all the other things that make ordinary cities:
        houses – comfortable; squares – treelined; shops – useful; services
        – functional; cafés and restaurants – convivial; sports grounds for
        adults, playgrounds for children; all the infrastructure necessary for
        a fluid, uncomplicated life. Roads would be curvilinear, tarmac
        smooth, glass doors and drawers would glide open with a sigh,

surfaces would be modulable, armchairs ergonomic.
And the physical existence of the city would be expanded in brochures and
articles trumpeting its success in five languages, maybe more.

There was nothing, there would be everything. That was their story.

The city was built. Its name was inscribed on topographical maps, added
to existing road signs and giving rise to new ones, all hurtling
towards its promises. Its name, Antipolis, was not an invention, it
was taken from an ancient city, founded many centuries before by
sailors from Greece. In their language, Antipolis meant 'the city
opposite', even though opposite their city there was only the sea.
The new Antipolis was constructed a few kilometres away from the place
where the first once stood – rather than being right on the shore, it
was set back among the trees. Its foundation stone was laid the
same year the Moderns walked on the moon. In spite of the physical
distance and the centuries that separated the two Antipolises, they
were propelled by the same impulse: that of modern civilisation, pro-
grammed to conquer, possess and exploit, to reduce the stranger to
nothing by planting one's flag there.

The Moderns dedicated hundreds of cities to the invention of their future.
Some of them were terribly important: there were innovations asso-
ciated with them, their reputations, their triumphs and the vestiges
of their sophisticated technologies remind us that modernity was
the next step towards man's mastering of the world. Antipolis was
one of these important cities – with its reputation, its triumphs –
but most of all,
it had a history.
Once upon a time, there was a man who built a city where there had been
nothing.
A story that begins like this forgets more than it remembers,
a story that begins like this is violent in its denial of the others, in its
dogged commitment to existing alone by establishing a domain of
which it then declares itself the sole owner,
but this is how the Moderns told it,

by burying,

by forgetting.

We don't know anything about the history that Antipolis erased in order to come into being – the scattered signs, imperceptible gestures, contrasting facts and conflicting facts, superimposed realities, distinctive voices and particular points of view –

all things without which a narrative is nothing other than the illusion of a world snapping to attention,

all things that the Moderns glossed over, so their stories would maintain their charming contours and elegant outlines, like polished machines. It didn't matter what had to be silenced, as long as their stories cleaved through the air, dazzled people, didn't explode upon take off, and if they did explode, they did it with panache, like a grand finale, because the love the Moderns had for beginnings was merely the lustrous figure in whose shadow was lodged their fear of – but also their desire for – violent endings: catastrophe, apocalypse, collapse, lockdown, destruction, devastation,

last day,

last hour,

last breath.

The Moderns began as builders, ended as tragedians.

We know that endings are as illusory as beginnings. They don't cleave neatly through the fabric of the world, they're embedded within things, within people, and they follow unpredictable trajectories –

they might come together or disperse,

accelerate or slow down,

pair up or pull away.

They're discrete, or multiple.

From its beginning to its end, the Moderns portrayed Antipolis as an interval between two ruptures.

Its beginning – an intentional rupture: there would be everything.

Its ending – an enforced rupture: the entire city destroyed at once. According to official history, there was a crisis, a crisis so terrible that after many years of expansion and prosperity, the city simply collapsed in one go. But whatever history might claim, the decline of Antipolis had begun long before the official date of its demise.

Buildings deserted,
offices emptied by night,
homes unoccupied, doors swinging on their hinges.
Without explanation.
Without any concern either, for rather than dealing with these abandon-
ments, rather than trying to put things right, the city simply went
elsewhere and carried on with the only activity it was capable of,
the only narrative available to it: beginning. No matter it was
destroying itself in one part of town, as long as it could enact the
same innovation a little further away, continue to announce new
buildings, new activities, projects, successes, inventions, feats, triumphs, numbers – higher, surface areas – bigger; no matter it was
falling into ruin, as long as it continued to announce new building
projects; and no matter, even, that the buildings were never completed and remained forever in a raw state of breeze blocks and
reinforced concrete.
Antipolis paid no more attention to its unfinished buildings than it did to
its deserted buildings – they were too scattered, too unimportant:
it was saving itself for the one that would outdo them all, the one
that would embody its downfall.
Eventually it came.
It was the biggest project Antipolis had ever seen. It was going to transform
the city, give it an image, because that's what it lacked, people said.
Antipolis might have had a name and a history, but it lacked an icon.
So an architect came up with the idea of a gigantic wave made of glass
and concrete to be built at the entrance to the city. True, Antipolis
wasn't by the sea, but nor was it far from it, and anyway, the architect explained, the city had been born as waves are born, appearing
on an empty horizon, rising up, unstoppable, unstopped, unceasingly
gaining in power: a wave, but a positive wave, the architect stressed,
not a threat but a promise to be embodied in his building.
The architect described a fluid, graceful, welcoming colossus.
The carcass of the unfinished construction that looms over the city today
looks like a jaw. Yawning, about to snap shut.
This was the site of Antipolis's final scene, when builders became
tragedians.

In the sheer vastness of the construction – tonnes of cement, tonnes of glass, tonnes of steel, tonnes of polluted soil extracted from the ground –

in the twists and turns of the project – tonnes of rows, controversies, petitions, delays, adjournments –

they witnessed a sign as imperious as a divine decree: something commanded them to stop, something thundered, 'It is the end' – and it was the end, the city was abandoned, declared dead, returned to the nothingness that had preceded its everything. The birth of Antipolis, the death of Antipolis – so thought the Moderns, yet that thought, when we examine it, sounds as bizarre to us as a language we don't know, have never heard coming out of anyone's mouth, about which all we know is once upon a time it existed, once upon a time it was spoken.

Antipolis, city of the future, became Antipolis, city of memory. Its buildings reveal to us the dreams the Moderns had about themselves – the dreams, language, words and stories that our culture had to escape in order to be born.

When we discovered Antipolis, there was nothing to dig up: everything was there in plain view, like the stage of a theatre abandoned in the middle of a performance.

Impassable roads, asphalt bulging with centuries-old roots.

Toppled statues in a debris-strewn piazza.

Buildings with broken windows, their ceilings caved in.

Edifices held up not so much by their masonry as by the tree trunks entwined around them.

A metal façade gleaming on a hillside that vanishes as soon as the sun goes down.

A bronzed glass cube rising out of a clearing. No window, no door to break its surface, it looks like a monolith that was built for the sole purpose of reflecting the world.

A concrete embankment rising up through the trees like a barricade. Along its top runs a road, straighter and wider than the others. The lower part of the wall is covered in multicoloured ornamentation. We transcribed what we found – LAK, KENY, Keny 2004, Bedo 2008, tcs, JBO, DREW NO, C-Den 2038 – but no one has yet come up with a convincing interpretation.

At the top of a hill stands a group of small orange buildings. This is where the inhabitants of Antipolis lived.

At first, we assumed that Antipolis had never been populated, that it was a utopia, abandoned as soon as it was built. Then we discovered a pile of photographs on the ground floor of one of the orange buildings. Initially, we couldn't make anything out, we had to have them translated for us. Then we realised we were looking at these same places peopled with men and women, we saw their faces, cheerful or serious, but invariably naïve – we saw them growing old and dying, and others succeeding them, we saw them change with each generation – clothes, hairstyles, bearing. The earliest inhabitants look self-conscious, as if they are following a script. A slightly apprehensive expression or pose suggesting the extent of their doubt – would this really make them seem modern? As time goes on their hesitation diminishes. They stop posing, grow confident, rapid, efficient, athletic, as they throw themselves into the quest for the future. Nothing can hold them back, not even a photograph.

Artefacts don't resolve unease, they displace it. Once these images had confirmed that Antipolis had indeed been inhabited – that it was a ghost city, rather than a stillborn city – the unease that its desolation had stirred in us turned into the unease of presence: how were we to think about these bodies, so distant and yet somehow familiar? What should we feel about them? The usual scorn we felt for the Moderns, for their blindness, their baseless self-confidence? Or compassion? These men and women, we see them running, going in and out of buildings, standing on podiums, speaking into microphones, raising their hands, applauding, we see them smiling, laughing, leaning over microscopes, looking at screens, driving vehicles, pointing cameras, identifying targets: they're constantly busy, but their energy resembles despair. Their endless motion is an avoidance mechanism that will not escape a thing.

Not long ago, one of the buildings in Antipolis collapsed.
An initial investigation concluded that the ground beneath it had opened up.
A second investigation revealed that Antipolis's limestone subsoil is

hollowed out by a maze of underground galleries and caves. Another city, its negative, is spread out beneath the first, imperilling it from the very beginning.

A third investigation concluded that the city only remains standing thanks to the tree roots entwined around its foundations. But they will eventually give way. The sea is rising. It has already swallowed the shoreline and the coastal towns, with their ramparts, alleyways and vestiges of antiquity. It has engulfed the forest, risen as far as Antipolis, and every day it is eroding the already fragile ground. The collapse of this building is merely the first sign and whichever build- ings don't collapse will eventually be submerged.

Should we save Antipolis?

This is the question that brings us together today.

It's not a question of capability or of means, for we know how to build barrages, we know how to make terrain solid and compact, we know how to raise the level of the ground, we even know how to move it from one part of the world to another.

We could save Antipolis.

The question is, should we?

If we were to preserve it, we would be acting like the Moderns, jealously guarding the city against its surrender to non-human forces. We would be doomed to repeat all those stories, words, ways of think- ing that we have tried so hard to escape.

Shouldn't we do to Antipolis what the Moderns were never able to do? Recognise that not everything depends on us,

capitulate

– not as one might declare an end –

but as one might offer a gift.

One of the Moderns' favourite legends was that of Atlantis. Once upon a time this island, this resourceful island-city, was colossal, prosper- ous, untouchable, and for all of these reasons it was punished and made to sink beneath the sea. No trace of it remains.

It's very tempting to think of Antipolis as the new Atlantis or, if we turn the myth into a prophecy, to think of Antipolis as an Atlantis foretold – for that's the allure of modern stories, reality always seems ready to bear them out. In the legend of Atlantis, men are everything. Even condemned men, even punished men – they are the centre around which revolve forces whose only purpose is to react to their facts, their actions and their thoughts.

Perhaps it is time to invent an Atlantis whose sinking would not be a punishment, but simply the beginning of an existence beyond our grasp.

Before other speakers follow me up onto this podium and we begin our discussion, I have something I would like to describe to you. It's neither a story nor a response to the question we are here to resolve. It's an image.

The glass wave that was to be the icon of Antipolis was the building nearest to the coast, and thus the first to be caught by the water. If the glass wave had been completed, there would have been a terrace on its crest. From there, visitors would have been able to see the forest spread out before them, trees interspersed with buildings, growing sparser and disappearing as they approached the shore. In the distance, held in the crook of the horizon, they would have been able to see the sea.

Today there is no forest opposite the wave, there are no more buildings, no more shore. The sea stretches as far as the eye can see,

white at daybreak,

blue at noon,

black at dusk.

It's easy to swim there. You do a few strokes and then, if you turn back to look at the shore, you see what the Moderns never imagined that eyes would ever see.

The hills of Antipolis, darkened by the pines that cover them,

the buildings of Antipolis, smoothed out by distance, their appearance pristine, nestled in the forest as if they were just another of its life forms,

the entire city reflected in the water.

In this reflection I realised that the stillness of Antipolis was just an illusion, for in the reflection I saw

the buildings brought to life by the sea,

I saw them breathing,

– slowly, carefully –
I saw them agree
to abandon their original image,
to enter their reflection,
to enter the movement;
I saw Antipolis slip inside its double, in the very place where no one ever
        built it.

MINOR

Marta
Michałowska

CHARACTERS

**September 2008,
ruins of the Tenth-Anniversary Stadium, Warsaw,
late morning**

He gets out of the cab of his tipper lorry. It'll be a while until the diggers fill up the bed. He slams the door, walks away from the vehicle, digs out a squashed, red packet of Caro's from the pocket of his hi-viz jacket and pulls out a crumbling cigarette. He searches for a lighter in his other pocket, lights the Caro and takes a long drag. He looks up at the mess all around. Three diggers are ripping remnants of the stands. The timber benches are long gone. They've been decaying since the early 1980s when the stadium was abandoned due to a technical fault, so they say. Apparently, the breaks in matches had to be half an hour long to accommodate a ten-minute walk each way between the changing rooms and the grounds.

He lets the cigarette ash fall onto the damp earth by his steel-toe-capped boots. There isn't even a blade of grass left of the former pitch. They trampled down the turf with lorry tyres, digger tracks and their boots. He turns around and looks at the earth mounds that have already been cleared off the remnants of the stands and the wild flowers that grew over them in the past twenty-five years. His granddad built this stadium together with a hundred and thirty thousand others. They say that they did the work in record time, over only eleven months. Granddad Edek was very proud of playing his part; he loved coming here.

He takes another long drag of his cigarette and looks towards the tunnel leading out of the stadium. He's been driving back and forth through it for days, with paving stones, railings, broken stairs and weeds on the back of the lorry. There won't be much left by the end of the week. That said, the mounds of earth and rubble that his granddad shovelled in 1954 will stay. They are going to build the new stadium on top of them. They will pour tonnes of concrete. That's the way things are done these days. They will put in plastic seats. And nice toilets, and bars, and cafés. And it will be all lovely and neat for a bit. And a few years down the line, they will let it rot again. And then, they will bring a wrecking ball or maybe even dynamite. A digger won't be enough to break up the tonnes of reinforced concrete.

He remembers the day when his granddad brought him here for the first time. It was on the eighth of September 1968, forty years ago almost to the day. It was a harvest festival, one of those grand communist occasions. Speeches, folk dance performances, music. Politicians, apparatchiks and them: ordinary Poles, working people, families. The stands were packed. They say that there were over one hundred thousand people here, even if the terraces were built to accommodate only seventy thousand. He sat in between his granddad and great-aunt Hania, Granddad Edek's older sister who worked at the offices of the Association of Polish Architects. She probably got them the tickets. There were some small privileges that came with her job.

He was only five years old, but he could never forget that man who set himself on fire right in front of him, yelling 'For our and your freedom.' He couldn't understand what was going on, but those words stayed with him. He had no idea what freedom was. His granddad pulled him away, dragged him up the steps and out of the stadium.

He'd never wanted to come back after that day, but then his mother got a job here, at the bazar – Jarmark Europa they called it – in the early 1990s. She was serving coffee from a trolley, wandering all day long in between market stalls set up on the crown of the stadium and within its car parks and grounds. The traders sold just about everything: from underpants to pirate videos, from trainers to contraband cigarettes, from Vietnamese pho to guns. There weren't many jobs around in those early years of capitalism, so his mum pushed the coffee trolley every single day, except Sundays and Christmas Day, for sixteen years. It was the largest bazar in Europe, so they say.

And now he is wrecking it all.

He finishes his cigarette, drops the butt into the mud and stamps it out with his boot.

November 1995,
Jarmark Europa, Tenth-Anniversary Stadium, Warsaw,
early morning

'Jadzia, give us a coffee. It's so cold this morning. My hands are frozen stiff already, and it doesn't look like it's going to get any warmer today.' A market trader specialising in women's tights and stockings from Turkey stops her as she makes her way down the alley between makeshift stands.

'Hey, Tomek. Winter is coming, again,' Jadzia replies and brings her cart to a halt. She takes a white plastic cup from a tall stack and places it on the counter, then reaches for a jar of Maxwell House instant coffee. Her rigid fingers, sticking out from red fingerless gloves, struggle with the blue lid. The jar slips and smashes against the grey tarmac. The fine brown granules spill, while the plastic lid rolls away down the alley. Her eyes follow it as it makes its way among the market stalls being piled with multi-coloured goods from all over the world: bedding, towels, plastic bowls and basins, t-shirts, jeans, socks, handbags, CDs, mobile phones, eggs, bananas, spring rolls, perfumes. On a day like today most traders erect gazebos and patio umbrellas over their wares. A chilly mist has set over the bazar and there is a fine drizzle in the air which clings to everything. The blue wheel of the coffee jar lid turns towards the left and disappears in the distance in the Vietnamese section.

Jadzia remembers her first day here. It felt as if she crawled into an ant nest. There were people busying themselves everywhere, people from all around the world. She'd never seen Africans or Asians before. At first, it all felt confusing, terrifying even: all these people with their strange languages and their strange foods simmering in huge pots out in the open. They haggled and did their deals as she struggled with her trolley loaded with a gas canister and a water boiler. She could hardly walk after ten hours of pushing it up and down the slope. Her muscles were so weak then. She had sat in her previous job in the factory, then the factory closed, just like many others at the time, transformations, they said, the economy needed to restructure, and unprofitable state-owned companies had to go, as the new Poland was coming, but nobody quite knew when and to whom. Then she sat at home, on the kitchen chair, thinking all day long how she would feed her three youngest with what was left of the starvation unemployment benefit the government gave her. It's much easier to push a cart filled with boiling water up the hill than tell a child that they can't have more dumplings, as there are none left. And these were just basic flour and potato *kopytka* with a few rings of fried onions and some parsley from the pot on the window sill. Her eldest two had their own families by then, and their own empty pots were screaming for better times they'd been promised. Mirek was collecting scrap and cardboard, pushing his own trolley through the streets of Warsaw.

'Not a good start, Jadzia. Is he going to charge you for that coffee?' asks Tomek with a note of sympathy in his voice, which feels genuine. Some of the other traders would take pleasure in her misfortune. She'll need to tell her boss later. It's better that way, even if she could easily make up for that half a jar. She is sure that somebody has seen it break and will mention it to the owner of the refreshments business. They don't look, but they see everything around here.

'I'm sure he will,' she responds, opening a fresh jar and placing two flat plastic teaspoons of the granules in the cup. She adds a spoon of sugar, bends down towards the boiler's tap to fill the cup with hot water, straightens, stirs the drink and hands it over to Tomek. He pays and she places the coins in the bag on her waist. This new money arrived only in January. There were no coins before. It's much easier to get confused with the small change, and they roll down the alleys fast when dropped, much faster than the jar lid. Then they disappear forever in someone's pocket.

'I can't get used to this new money. I miss being a millionaire,' she says zipping up the bag.

'We are just poor now, working for little coins. Before I used to bring ten million home at the end of the day, sometimes even twenty.'

8 September 1968,
Tenth-Anniversary Stadium, Warsaw,
Harvest Festival, noon

He yawns broadly. His jaw clicks. Maybe he should be more careful. Apparently, it's very painful when the jaws get locked, and you need to get someone to punch you to get your mouth shut again. But he can't help it. These events go on and on. He doesn't understand why they broadcast them to the whole country. At least the weather is good and he doesn't have to freeze his arse off. But he can't bear all these hours of folk dancing. And the speeches. It's unreal that some people have so much to say to go on for five hours. And you are stuck on the same shot. Medium closeup. That's it. Occasionally you check if the First Secretary of the Worker's Party or some other apparatchik didn't get out of focus, while they go on and on, punctuating their speech with, 'Comrades, citizens, workers, we can look into the future with confidence, because we are on the right path, because we have the right friends and allies, and we are guided by the immortal idea of socialism...' And you wish that idea died and together with it the interminable speech, even if you would never utter these thoughts out loud. And sometimes you worry that they can read your mind, especially in those moments when you are imagining the First Secretary having a sudden heart attack and dropping dead, and finally finishing his oration.

But he isn't filming any of that today. His job is to get the crowds. What are all these people doing here on such a beautiful Sunday? He would go for a swim in the river. It might be the last chance this year. It's September already. Another yawn comes out of him. He looks at his watch. It's only quarter past noon. This is going to be a long day.

'Camera 3, pan right from the entrance tunnel, along the lower rows of the stands,' the director instructs him through the headset.

He looks through the camera viewfinder. There is some commotion going on to the right of the entrance to the pitch in sector number 37. He zooms the camera in. There is a gap in the crowd. People are rushing away. There is a little boy in a centre of the frame, no older than five, his mouth wide open, his eyes huge. He looks as if he has been struck by a lightning. An older man pulls him away, his grandfather perhaps.

Two rows down, a man with a large moustache and a beret is on fire. Other men try to put him out with their jackets. They knock him over. But he gets up and the other men disperse. He is yelling. But it's impossible to make out the words from here, over the folk music that carries on playing. In the foreground, the dancers continue with their performance.

He zooms his camera in as far as he can.

The man is engulfed in flames.

A policeman appears in the frame.

Someone tries to extinguish the man again.

He tries to keep the burning man in the centre of the frame, the focus fixed on his face. The man is still saying something. He lifts his arms above his head. His fists are clenched.

The flames are starting to die down.

More policemen move into the frame. They obscure the burning man.

The man's face keeps on reappearing in between them.

The flames are extinguished.

The man's shirt and beret are gone. His hands are black. There is a dark stain on his skin all over his neck and chest. He disappears in a crowd that has gathered around him, now that he is no longer ablaze.

He searches for the man's face through the camera viewfinder. He spots him. The man looks as if he is gasping for air. He feels that he catches the man's glance through the camera lens.

'Camera 3, are you asleep? Pan right, I said. Move on.'

September 1954, between Saska Kępa and Old Praga, by the river Vistula, Warsaw, early morning

He can feel drops of sweat rolling down his back from in between his shoulder blades. The earth he is shovelling is heavy. They asked them to bring old Warsaw here. Truckload after truckload, cartload after cartload, what is left of his city keeps on arriving. They want them to mix it with soil to form earth mounds for the new stadium.

These are our houses. These were our houses.

Next year on the twenty-second of July, they will sit on them, listening to one of the leaders of the new Poland unfolding his vision for the better life ahead, slowly, over many hours. Maybe they will invite him. They say a workers' paradise is being built. The future is bright for the labouring man. Soon they will be moving into new flats with toilets inside and baths and communal heating, that's what they've been told. He can't wait to have a hot bath. But for now, a bucket has to do.

Sometimes tears come to his eyes as he shovels. A fragment of a green glazed brick with a vine pattern catches his eye, or a broken mosaic floor tile, or a piece of blood red glass from a stained-glass window. They've been shovelling remnants of their walls, floors and ceilings. The war had turned everything into a pile of rubble. There was little left standing. He walked up and down the streets of his city throughout the autumn of 1944. It was as if he had woken up in an apocalypse. Everything was grey. Thick dust settled over ruins. He felt as if he were the sole survivor. As he walked among the charred and blown-up remnants, he would smell turnips being boiled. He would follow his nose and find a group of people gathered around an open fire, a blackened pot simmering above the flames.

They all camped in the ruins of their houses. Some found saucepans or cups that survived, or a loose photograph, or a book with only lightly charred covers. Everyone sieved through dust and rubble for even the smallest untouched fragment of the life before. He carries in his pocket a piece of a green glass vase painted with a pattern of water lilies that belonged to his mother. That's all he has left of her.

This year, September is hotter than August. His vest is already drenched, and it's still early. They haven't taken their first break yet. He is thirsty. His mouth is coated in dust floating up from the mounds of rubble being unloaded from the constantly arriving trucks and carts. He slips off his right glove and wipes sweat from his forehead with the back of his hand to stop it rolling into his eyes and stinging them. It's hard to imagine a perfect oval stadium with sloping seating, a VIP stand, a football pitch and an athletics track from this perspective. He squints as he gazes around. In the early morning sun workers like him are shovelling all around.

'Hey, Edek. Stop dreaming and keep shovelling.' He hears the voice of the foreman right behind him. That one wants to see all his men with bent backs all the time. He thinks they don't deserve to be *Homo Erectus*, and is leading them to the next stage of evolution: *Homo Sovieticus*. A regression. But what can Edek say? He snatches another glance at the building site, puts his glove back on and picks up his shovel.

'Leave fantasising to the architects. Come on, otherwise we won't finish on time and they will hang us by our balls,' the foreman adds and walks away.

July 1953,
offices of the Association of Polish Architects, Warsaw,
late afternoon

She holds her breath as she pushes the door open with a tray laden with clean cups and a pot of fresh coffee. If she didn't know there was a jury meeting going on in the room, she would drop the tray and run screaming, 'Fire, fire!' The thirteen men around the table are enveloped in dense smoke. The open window isn't helping much with clearing the air in the room. The windless heat of this year's infernal summer makes the hanging cigarette fumes feel even more like fire smoke. But the architects and the representatives of the ministries don't seem to be bothered. Occasionally some cough, but with so much talking they need to clear their throats from time to time. They have taken their jackets off, rolled up their sleeves and most loosened their ties by now. They have large circles of perspiration under their armpits.

They don't notice her as she walks in. She puts the tray on a side table. None of them turn around. She doesn't mind. They need to focus on the important task at hand. They must select the winning project by the end of the day. And there isn't much left of the working day. It doesn't look like they will finish before supper. She might need to bring them sandwiches and cold cuts in a few hours. The smoke tickles her throat and she coughs, unable to suppress the urge. She places her hand on her mouth. She's never smoked in her life, but must have inhaled nicotine and tar from thousands of cigarettes since she got the job in the office here, especially during competition judging. And there have been a fair few of those in recent years. So much needs to be built in the poor Warsaw that is still rising from the ashes. The future of their capital is being defined here in this room. These men have quite a job in front of them.

She picks up a porcelain cup and saucer from the tray, fills it with coffee and walks over to the table. Her eyes search for the best place to put it safely among the architectural drawings spread out and rolled all over the huge table. She gazes over the black ink outlining visions for the national stadium to be built on the other side of the Vistula to mark ten years since the declaration of the Twenty-second of July Manifesto and the formation of the Polish People's Republic. Some say that Stalin wrote that manifesto himself, but he is dead now and all sorts of things are being said that nobody dared to utter before. She has her favourite project. She had a good look when they went for lunch.

'But Comrades, we have to remember that architecture must support the transformation of society. This is not about what is pleasing,' says one of those government people that usually comes here to join the architects for the more important competitions. She is not sure what transformation he's talking about exactly. The war ended not long ago and everything has been changing ever since. The whole city is a huge building site. Not that there was much of it left. Everyone is desperate for new houses. She no longer cares whether the new Warsaw will be beautiful or ugly. And who is she to say what beauty is. It all changed. All she is sure about is that the old Warsaw was beautiful.

'Comrade is certainly right, but all these proposals largely fulfil the correct ideology. And we still need to select the winner,' one of the architects says in response. And he is right. They've been here since eight in the morning and all seven proposals are still on the table. They keep on rolling and unrolling them and not a single one has been dismissed so far. She puts the cup in front of the architect and reaches for the ashtray overflowing with ash from his almost empty packet of Caro cigarettes. Where did he manage to get these?

'Largely! Comrade doesn't seem to fully appreciate the responsibility that rests on our shoulders. This stadium will be there to last and propagate the vision of the only right doctrine,' the official from the ministry shouts across the table.

She empties the ashtray, puts it back down and carries on serving coffee, moving clockwise around the table. Not one of the men thanks her. She is here as if she were not. And she will be for many more hours and many more cups of coffee and perhaps some brandy later.

'Absolutely. I completely agree with Comrade. Even more so, we must select the proposal that brings beauty to the citizens of Warsaw and those that will come from all around the world to attend sporting competitions,' the architect replies taking a long drag from his Caro cigarette. He blows a huge grey cloud across the table over the drawings.

'I don't understand why Comrade keeps on going on and on about charming aesthetics. We are creating national norms here and they need to be easily understood by the masses. There is no room for frivolities,' snaps back the official loosening his narrow red tie. He is the last still wearing one.

She pours a cup of coffee, walks towards him and looks for a space in front of him to place it among the drawings he has pulled closer to himself. She recognises the proposals. They are not that exceptional.

'So what criteria does Comrade propose to move forward with the judging of the projects in front of us?' asks the architect and stands up. He leans over the drawings, his cigarette hanging off his lower lip. Ash drops over the designs.

'We have no choice over criteria, Comrade,' shouts the apparatchik, flinging his arms up into the air. 'Social Realism is the only way forward for architecture,' he adds, gesticulating wildly.

She stands beside him, to his right, the cup still in her hand. One of the younger architects from their association, sitting a couple of seats to the left of the ministry official, whispers into his colleague's ear but loud enough for everyone to hear, 'But Stalin is dead, they could let us breathe.'

The ministry man drops his hands onto the table, shifts in his chair and leans to the left, towards the whispering architect. Silence falls in the room. The young man freezes like a naughty schoolboy. His face turns red.

This is her moment. The path to the table is clear. She leans forward to place the cup down.

'And what does Comrade propose? Shall we go back to degenerate avant-garde, empty formalism, imperialist schematism? With or without our great leader, Comrades, you must remember you are engineers of the human soul. Architecture is not about individualist self-expression, or breathing as Comrade put it.' He seems quite agitated and stands up suddenly, knocking the coffee cup filled to the brim from her hand. The dark brown liquid splashes all over the drawings like a giant inkblot.

'And what have you just done, woman!' The apparatchik turns around towards her, his face as red as his tie.

She can feel her body freeze. Everyone shifts their gaze from the apparatchik to look at her. Nobody says anything. She feels all thirteen pairs of eyes burning her. She would like to melt like a snowman and become nothing more than a wet stain on the floor.

Smoke snakes up towards the ceiling from lit cigarettes resting in ashtrays all around the table. The Caro smoking architect, standing on the other side of the table, reaches for his cigarette, lifts it to his lips and takes a drag. Nobody else moves. He blows the smoke out and looks at the cigarette in his hand.

'Perhaps Mrs Hania has solved the Gordian knot,' he says breaking the silence in the room.

All the eyes shift towards him.

'Those four proposals were nothing special anyway. Let's get them out of here,' he continues as he takes another long drag from his Caro, and then puts it back down in the ashtray. He leans forward across the table and starts gathering the stained paper. He folds and crushes the drawings into a ball and throws them on the floor behind him.

The apparatchik looks in disbelief, but doesn't raise objections. Perhaps he wants to go home in time for supper after all. There are still three more proposals in the competition rolled out on the other side of the table.

'Dear Hania, while we are at it, perhaps you would like to come over here,' adds the architect, crushing the cigarette stump in the ashtray.

She walks around the table and, once there, tries to reach for the architect's cup to refill it. He grabs her arm.

'I don't want any more coffee,' he tells her.

She straightens and looks at him. No doubt he'll fire her now in front of everyone. She holds her breath.

'Hania, you've been here with us all day. I'm sure you had a good look at all the proposals?'

She nods in response, and immediately regrets her honesty. Curiosity is rarely rewarded.

'Perhaps you have a favourite one?'

She nods again. There is no point in lying now.

Everyone's eyes are on her again.

'What are you doing, Comrade?' asks the apparatchik.

The architect looks towards the government official and takes the last Caro from the packet in front of him. Without shifting his gaze, he crushes the empty, red packet into a ball and drops it back onto the table. Then he picks up his lighter and brings its flame to the tip of the cigarette in between his lips. Everyone around the table is following his every movement. The architect inhales, holds the smoke down for a minute or two as he looks around the room, his expression impenetrable.

He finally exhales a series of hazy circles and replies, 'Letting one of the masses decide.'

Then he turns towards her and asks, 'So, which one is it?' He smiles warmly and nods with encouragement.

WORD

translated from Arabic by Mona Kareer

The horizon bustled with buildings, stacked up, side by side, before each other. The lines of their walls, balconies, and roofs merged, and at first impression, they composed labyrinths of occult words. Before this crammed display, lacking in colour, stretched across the radar's screen, the engineer sat attentively, trying to decode whatever words these buildings had written. Sometimes, the display registered movements of individuals, whom the distance turned into sombre shadows of no words. The only sound accompanying them was the rustle of the engineer's clothes whenever he moved, or the weight of his fingers on the keyboard attached to the radar, which revealed the lack of synchronisation between what appeared on the screen and what could be heard inside the room. This discord between the seen and the heard became yet more evident when suddenly a sombre shadow appeared on a balcony of one apartment in a grand building, while the only sound came from the chair on which the engineer sat scratching the floor, followed again by the sound of his fingers as they pressed the keyboard to enlarge the image, looking into the western side of the balcony, where the sombre shadow leaned for a few seconds before disappearing again inside the apartment. It seemed to be a pot plant. And it was only in that moment that the engineer spotted the word 'sSEsamE' written by the lines of the building, drawing from the end of that balcony, across another balcony, long and narrow without a frame, linked to a stairway, followed by a similar balcony and a stairway. 'sSEsamE'. Sesame.

This word has never been innocent or neutral since her first appearance five thousand years ago when she began to pull her tricks on the heavenly world, starting from the Kingdom of Ugarit, where some took to rubbing themselves in her oil to wash off the blood of their victims at times, to cleanse away their sins, says the Myth of Ba'al, as did Anat, the goddess of war and hunting, following her battle with Mot, the god of death, and at other times, to make babies during the rituals of the fertile night before Nikkal, the goddess of the moon, says the Hurrian Songs, after which this went on and on for centuries up until the night after the seven-hundredth night of the one thousand and one nights. There, it was not only that Shahrazad made use of the word 'sesame' in narrating a story during her rituals of enchanting Shahryar, out-manoeuvring her possible death, or that Ali Baba repeated the word when thieving the thieves, but even

Antoine Galland took her into his French translation, adding another story to the delight of his readers, increasing the number of nights to get it closer, even if slightly, to one thousand and one nights.

But tricks pulled by gods and sorcerers, storytellers and translators, and the buildings that shelter their words, would not work on an engineer of his like, whose mission was to rebuild the forces of the literary language, and to change the standing structures of narrative: 'Ouvre-toi, boom boom.' The keyboard responded by activating orders for the intelligent target system to launch a missile at the building. In a matter of minutes, the target was neutralised, the word was erased, and the collateral damage was estimated at level 1, where a single victim was confirmed, interrupted while caring for their pot plant. Except for that one, there was no reason to believe other casualties would be registered among civilians, given no one emerged from underneath the ruins, which appeared on the radar's screen as a pile of sand and concrete and iron bars, looking like a gap in the flesh that an extracted tooth leaves in the jaw, a gap for light. Light suddenly poured between the buildings, inscribing a rectangle of twisted lines on the rubble. The engineer stood up and stretched back and forth, left and right. It was necessary for someone whose job required sitting before a screen for long hours, as in the case of the engineer, as well as the writer, to do some exercises for about a quarter of an hour daily. He then returned to his seat, with energy and vigour, revived by the renewal of his blood circulation across the body and the deep breaths he took.

The engineer directed the monitoring lenses towards a group of buildings at the centre of the screen, moving between the lines they had drawn, trying to decode more words, until he was stopped by the large building of a mosque with two minarets making the word 'MaY.' Since it was an expression of doubt, he let it be. And as per the master of words Abū al-ʿAlāʾ Aḥmad ibn ʿAbd Allāh ibn Sulaymān al-Tanūkhī al-Maʿarrī, known as Abū al-ʿAlāʾ al-Maʿarrī, 'The sole certainty is that there is no certainty, my best effort is to suspect and predict,' in contradiction to Ibn al-Athir who refers to 'MaY' not on the side of suspicion and prediction, but as 'perhaps', the way Imru' al-Qais says, 'perhaps our fates have come to more misery.' Following some further evaluation, though, another boom would be heard, taking down the minaret on the right side of the mosque. After all, it was written as 'May' not 'MaY,' says the dictionary. Meanwhile, the sun continued to expose the minaret's dust as it attempted to settle on the roofs of neighbouring buildings. No doubt the collateral damage in human souls would be estimated at level 1, given the shift to modern sound technology to announce the calls for prayer in place of a real person. As for the stones that went flying in every direction, cracking the windows of some neighbouring buildings, they could not possibly cause high damage in human souls. The flying stones could neither be considered a lethal weapon, nor were they meant to be one. The engineer had had no intention to make them crack the windows. And in the absence of an intention, it was not possible to accuse someone of a war crime. Therefore, it could be said that in such cases overall, if there were damage among civilians, such damage was not part of the damage that may be officially recognised as collateral. It was only a matter of a technical error. Still, despite levelling the minaret and parts of the letter 'M', the word now appeared more like 'Hay', and since there could be no room for linguistic confusion here, the word had to be fixed immediately, even back to a normal 'may'. Usually for this type of target high-precision weapons are needed. And so it went, a smart bomb flew towards the top of the mosque's dome, elegantly devouring her. Now that was a proper word, surrounded by the plunging rubble of the building's left side, removed a few seconds ago, like the stain left by a penciled word erased from paper. The cast lead, the ruined concrete, the spilled sand had come to crown the word 'may' as it stood now distinctly among the buildings. And to make things clearer, a new series of missiles went off, erasing all the lines drawn by the surrounding buildings, so 'may' was left alone in a square turned almost yellow by the missiles, rubble, and sand, the colour of recycled paper. This time, the engineer could not possibly predict the damage in human souls, which made no appearance on the radar's screen, but his estimate rose from level 1 to level 2, considering the number of buildings bombed.

The next steps for the engineer's linguistic intervention in the constructed space relied essentially on what followed the word 'may' in one's literary intuition. And here she went, the mighty intuition, swearing by the name of god, all on her own, declaring right in the moment: 'may he be striking,' which was to say, 'he continues to strike down.' And so it went, the display on the screen changing every few seconds.

Remote-controlled weapons. Guided missiles. Precision-guided munitions. Smart bombs. Laser pods. Eco-friendlier than traditional weapons, with a cost of production less than the price of one bullet. Hitting the targeted building and destroying it within five seconds. Targeting any building in the order of whatever words appear in the moment. The possibility of civilian casualties. A technical error. Taking charge of the remote-controlled weapon station. The engineer's ability to make judgment while taking into consideration the estimated level of damage in civilians against linguistic advantage. The engineer's ability, not that of the radar's or the autonomous weapons systems', to make judgment based on language and grammar standards. The engineer's ability to develop a distinct literary instinct that allowed him to make a decision on the use of force in certain circumstances, in view of the radar's screen and the smart target system's failure, despite their smartness, to comprehend the idea of punishment, or the possibility of deterrence by punishment. Collateral damage on level 1. Collateral damage on level 2. Collateral damage on level 3. Gradually. The ability to activate total power in the blink of an eye. The ability to be monstrous to the point that the radar's screen becomes almost a blank page, stained by erased words, until Shahrazad ceases to say her permitted words.

The engineer turned off the devices, slightly pushed his chair back, stood up, switched off the light, and closed the door behind.

Now that all the set language shapes and literary forms have been erased, the floor has become ready for the engineering teams to rebuild the place and the language, to pour in their concrete and ink so they may draw their more contemporary literary line, which has no past to lean back on, or a present to entertain, only a unique future awaiting ahead.

THE BLIND

SPOT

Alia Trabucco Zerán

translated from Spanish by Sophie Hughes

José was the first to quit. His reason: a fifteen-year-old boy, the skin on his cheeks still smooth, his eyes black and misty, just like my son's eyes only wide open, wide, wide open, José repeated through dry lips and with white, encrusted spittle at the corners of his mouth.

Victoria was the next to go. Her motive: a woman who looked a hundred but was barely fifty, her body wrecked from so much toil, back bent double, calloused hands and every one of her teeth, so many teeth, shattered against the floor. Like smashed pieces of china, Victoria muttered, her gaze fixed on the floor tiles, as if the fragments were still there, as if they would haunt her forevermore.

Then it was Alex's turn, then Vilma, Ximena, Omar and Brian, although no one called him Brian – he hated that gringo name – but B. B only lasted a month and a day, and they nicknamed him B the Brief, all because of that pregnant lady and the mob of journalists who got inside his head like a buzzing in the ears: had he seen her or not, was she facing forwards or backwards when she jumped, did he hear a scream or just the thud, oh my my my, the thud against the floor.

Six months, three months, sometimes they didn't even last as long as that. It was deceptive, that job. *Cleaning responsibilities*, the ad said, as if it made no difference what you clean: shit, dust, hair, blood. But one of the staff did stick it out year after year, body after body. Her name was Roxana Paredes and behind her back they called her La Original.

Her age: unknown, although people said she was around forty. Her height: tall to some, short to a few and average to most. Reddish hair, no dispute there, red like fire, and her lips were cracked from so many years spent in the dry air confined between those walls. Rumour had it she'd been there since day one, hence the nickname. People said the floor had gleamed at the grand opening from her painstaking mopping, and that when the manager cut the ribbon to inaugurate the tallest mall on the continent, La Original slipped out among the guests and secretly picked it up. That ribbon is a lucky charm, her colleagues would whisper behind her back, a talisman tucked in between the deodorant and a statue of Our Lady of

Andacollo; although others would say there was no statue, no locker, and that La Original must have been a crackpot because only crackpots don't crack up in the end.

It's not clear whether she was aware of her own nickname, or if she ever heard the legend of the veteran cleaning lady, the one who washed down the bloodstained floor tiles, the one who didn't fear the drop. It's not clear if she knew that story was about her and all the deaths she'd endured: eighty men, a hundred women, some elderly people, and even one child. She would carry on with her routine of bleach, silence, and window cleaner, and it was always her voice that raised the alarm at suicide hour. Code en-four, en-four, her colleagues would hear over their portable radios, quickly turning them off or repeatedly pretending not to have heard. But in the end, someone would always take pity and trundle down to the ground floor to confirm the tragedy of yet another victim in the reflection of the shop windows.

Maybe she enjoys it, some whispered, different strokes for different folks, but you only had to see the way she broke down when they all went home. No one understood how she did it, or why she'd stayed on all those years, after all those deaths, and there was even talk about how she had some-thing to do with the falls. But others said: no way, La Original is weird but she's no murderer, and they defended her integrity, reminding the bad-mouthers of the fact as solid as the walls of that building: bread's bread, they would say, and money's money, who were they to judge the redhead for sticking around. The truth was that she did once get the urge to quit, or that's what those bitchy people say. One ordinary summer's afternoon as she was unbuttoning her uniform, she felt a tingling just above her eyebrows. They say she paused for a moment, blinked in bemusement, and if someone had asked her in that moment why she'd gone so pale, what was upsetting her, she would have told them: I just got my first wrinkle, in the middle of my forehead. But no one ever spoke to her, no one ever paid any attention to her face, so instead she went down to the ground floor alone with her pale complexion and her new crack.

Time was hazy in that place. Neither Omar nor Vilma ever put it like that, but if someone had asked them how many months they had worked in the mall of infinite escalators, they would have shrugged their shoulders and answered with a silence. There is no day or night in there, no inside or outside, only windows and steel and floor tiles and displays and that music playing on loop, with no beginning and no end. On the other hand, if someone had asked La Original how long she'd been in the building, she would have answered: seven years, nine months, two weeks, four days.

Her role was clear in that labyrinth of window displays: mop, disinfect, air-freshen, disappear, although some said she also attended the cleaning job interviews, where she would listen to the applicants' names and surnames and try to pick out the lies: fake enthusiasm, fake cheerfulness, fake experience, nothing got past her. But a debt's a debt, and a job's a job, so they all feigned commitment to the role and promised to be disciplined while La Original predicted the exact date each of them would leave.

It was at one such interview that she first saw David, even if he didn't recall the encounter. Spiked-up hair, thick lips, a piercing in his eyebrow. She felt as if she already knew him, that she'd seen him somewhere, but she didn't know from where, or when, and she gave up trying to remember. David came from Calama and apparently shared a room with a cousin. He was a good liar, full of smiles, although she sensed a sadness in him. La Original gave him three months at a push, and she wondered who his trigger would be: a new mum, a depressed teen, or maybe just a kid like him, little less than a man, little more than a boy.

That same week she found him hiding away in the food court. On seeing his face, now covered in a rash, she corrected her initial assessment: he probably wouldn't last a month. She was coming out of the staff locker room, her eyes itching, when she spotted him huddled at a table greedily eating an ice cream. At first she couldn't believe what she was seeing, it wasn't his turn working that floor, but even through her smarting eyes, she recognised his uniform and anguish. She sidled up to him – who did this kid think he was? – but as she drew nearer, she realised that the entire scene had happened before. Deja-vu, she said to herself, is the very pinnacle of bad luck; to have each day play out several times, as if one life weren't enough. La Original usually worked the ground level, in Falabella, and from there she would let her colleagues know if there was any news from the floor. But she knew that the food court was the best place to hide away in that building and, driven by a sudden wave of tiredness, she sat down opposite the kid.

David jumped and then pretended not to have seen her, but since she had him cornered, he said: no eyes here, boss, take it easy. She blinked, unsure which eyes he was referring to, until he pointed with his ice cream above their heads, to the dropped ceiling. They both looked up together, strangely choreographed: he with his big, droopy eyes, she with her two burning coals. Together they saw the steel, the halogen lights, the ceiling, and the absence of camera lenses, of spies: their secret was safe.

The blind spot, they called it, and they never had to fix a time: their meetings always began at six because that was the time of day that drove them crazy. Six is the most sinister time in that windowless building, the weary, despondent hour, the hour of last-minute offers, the hour of the dead. At six the halls become packed and the thermostats break down, the elevators stop suddenly and you can hear faint echoes and wailing. A chill spreads through the place and the ceiling lights go out, while children run away from their parents and get their fingers crushed on escalators. Every day, at that time, David would wait for her at the same table, while someone plunged from the top floor, driven by grief or despair.

They spent several evenings like that when it dawned on her that her absence made no difference. What's another blocked toilet. What's another overflowing bin. What's another sticky fingerprint on a shop window. La Original would switch off her portable radio and rub her itchy eyelids while the minutes of that eternal and fateful hour dragged by.

At first they didn't talk much, she held back, but David began to relax and slowly share his secrets. I'm going to be a jockey, he told her one evening, and she pictured him at a party, but he explained that he meant riding a colt that shot out of the starting gates like a star. He was scrawny, David, not ugly but not handsome either, with a black mole on his cheek which made him look almost distinguished. Sometimes he would turn up for work late and looking haggard, and he'd say, Roxi, don't rat on me, and he would tell her about his night and what he charged for a kiss. He had smooth, hairless arms, a fragile neck like a deer, long, bony fingers, and a voice that came from far away. David wanted to move to the countryside, plant rows of peach trees, have two foals and four greyhounds, which were like dwarf-sized horses. She liked the part about the dogs and asked about the colour of their coats: grey like shadows, he told her, and she immediately thought of the grey of concrete floor tiles.

Sometimes she would close her red eyes and strain to imagine herself with the kid and picture the greyhounds sprinting through a velvety meadow. She would brush their coats, feed them apple cores, weave them collars so no one could ever steal them. So many evenings went by like this, in raptures, while they talked about everything and nothing and managed to put the suicides to the back of their minds. She tried not to love him, she wasn't interested in making a new friend, but despite herself she walked through that door and lost the key that opened it. He called her: Roxi, Fire Eyes, and she: Silly Kid, and they would bicker about the names of their dogs: Ripley, Gucci, Nike and Prada.

That's what they were doing one evening, at the furthest, darkest table, when David pointed at a woman with his ice cream and said: there goes one of our lot. La Original didn't understand what he was talking about, what connected the three of them, so she looked at him, then at the woman, then at herself, somewhat perplexed. The kid was twenty years old, and he worked night and day, he preferred older men, liked chocolate and vanilla best. She couldn't see much of the woman, just the back of her head poking out from around a corner, red hair, very slim, she could be anyone, even La Original herself. And as for La Original, what could she say connected them? The answer startled her and she rubbed her feverish eyes.

They didn't go into that, not that day, why get bogged down in sadness. They merely heard the sigh, the heavy impact with the floor and then the jarring music and the announcement of a flash sale on household appliances. He wanted to say something but he didn't. Her eyelids blinked over her ember eyes. But if he had asked her what she was thinking, why that woman, what her reason had been, La Original would have answered: grief, tiredness, pain and debt.

That's how their evening ritual would start, as if they were counting sheep. Roxana sometimes guessed right, but David's gift was undeniable. It could be a sad old lady, a man in a suit or a young woman, and David would point and say: there goes another one ready for take-off. It was a short, sharp step, a lethal dance, a climb up and then the plummet like a rock into the abyss. It didn't seem to affect him and La Original started to question her original estimation: maybe he'll stay forever, maybe he'll keep me company in this life. Two peas in a pod, people said about them; thick as thieves, the bad-mouthers, although to her mind they were flower and fragrance, sun and warmth, tree and nest.

She was happy, La Original, although she would never have admitted it, they say she would bring David homemade *sopaipillas* which he would demolish. Days went by in that calm, and he lost all notion of time, but Roxana could quantify her happiness to precisely five weeks. It was that bitter winter, dry and cold like a black desert night. Maybe the climate disagreed with David and brought back bad memories. He stopped laughing, stopped talking about the foals, he would sit and stare silently into the void. She never asked about why he'd left, what he'd fled from up there in the north, but a shadow fell across his face to some memory that still haunted him.

Maybe it was the dry air, the dehydration biting at his lips, or all the harried people in those freezing cold halls. David began to drag his feet, he no longer wanted to eat ice cream and she could no longer draw him out of the darkness settling over him. Tell me about the countryside, she begged him, tell me about the foals and the greyhounds, but the kid only wanted to talk about the vastness of the skyscraper and whether she thought it was a dignified way to go, as swift and certain as a gunshot; or whether they would get vertigo, a sign that it was a mistake, a careless oversight. She would insist on changing the subject, close her bloodshot eyes and ask him to be quiet or to go and disinfect the urinals.

David hadn't been himself for days, his cuticles were bleeding from the constant nail biting, and even when she tried to take his restless hands in hers, she only met with resistance. Her eyes also grew worse, as if they were anticipating a great sadness, but that didn't occur to her straight away, and no one else seemed to notice.

That's where they were at one evening, as still and silent as statues, when a distant tune reminded her where she knew him from. She should never have told him, it's never a good idea to dredge up buried memories, but she felt such intense distress it was like the words had set her alight.

I dreamt about you, she told David, her voice shrunken from fear. It was just before I met you but I've only just remembered. He frowned distractedly, already somewhere else, somewhere far away, while Roxana studied that face which, some time ago, had woken her from her sleep. She considered telling him about her visions: I used to know you, you came to drag me with you, you can't pull the wool over my eyes, tell the truth. She didn't go into the details with him, she was frightened of somehow invoking that tragedy, but she couldn't now erase the image that had startled her in her dream. David let out a laugh and cried: Roxi, the clairvoyant! and he didn't want to hear about her nightmare or guess at the next dead person.

He left her sitting alone at their table and went to polish the water fountains, but she couldn't calm down after her dark premonition. She didn't notice anything strange about him that afternoon, just slowness, lethargy, but the next day she followed him around with her heart in pieces. David mopped the floor with bleach, replaced burned out bulbs, buffed the handrails till they shone and directed disoriented shoppers. He didn't meet her as usual at the blind spot, he glanced at her from one corner of the food court, and she swallowed saliva as bitter as the traces of her nightmare.

In the meantime, life, or rather death, went on, and Aron and Camila resigned, Mauro and Antonella walked out. Two thirty-year olds, wrapped in an embrace, jumped from Starbucks and a forty-year-old man shouted *look at me* then *enough* in mid-flight. La Original went back to the lingerie floor and to cleaning the toilets in Falabella, and would even repeat the en-four code in her decisive voice from the old days.

She often doubted herself, don't be stupid, she would say, one thing's a dream and another is this crappy reality. But she was no longer calm, she moved about clumsily and depressed, gazing angrily at the floor with those blazing eyes of hers, those bonfire eyes. She wandered lost around the footwear floor, walked right into an old lady, and was dazzled by the pale light of the blaring screens. She was in a world of her own, La Original, and could only see signs of danger: slippery floors, broken escalators, voltage collapses. She noticed her eyes were getting worse, increasingly dry and inflamed, and that all the palm trees were fake and the building had no exit. What time is it, she wondered, when will this hell be over, and what was going on with her eyes, what calamity did they presage.

One afternoon she lost sight of him and immediately feared the worst, but she found David wiping the ketchup in the food court. She stormed over to him and said, irritated: where did you disappear to, kid, tell me what's wrong, what happened to you, why won't you come back to the blind spot? David was wiping the tacky crust while quietly humming a tune, and he couldn't hear La Original who was still lecturing him, running out of patience. Bloody kid, she went on, speak when you're spoken to, but it took a clip over the ear for him to listen.

David took out his earphones, turned around painfully, and wrung the red-soaked cloth in his bruised hands. His face was wasted, he had a black eye and split lip, the piercing had been ripped from his eyebrow and there was a big slash where his mole was. La Original looked away. It was impossible, unthinkable, but she knew that devastated face, it had already been branded on her retina. He looked at her tenderly, like back when they used to imagine a future together, and he said: My Roxi, fading flame, and he planted a kiss in the middle of her forehead. Still and silent, Roxana watched him disappear down the hall, and she touched her wrinkle, the crack, and wished she'd never met him.

At six she went up to their table, collapsed into her chair and with her lava eyes, her terrifying eyes, she kept a watch over the blind spot in silence. It wasn't long before she heard the thud, as sharp and decisive as any, and then a ringing in her ears, and she suddenly felt dizzy. She blinked several times, stunned, until she regained her composure and said over to herself, that's enough, calm down, you always knew what was coming. She stood up after a while, strode over to the railing and leaned over the edge to confirm her suspicion. Although afraid, Roxana took a deep breath and looked down. An icy breeze shot through her.

There was no tent yet, just the body on the floor tiles and a heady silence like the one they say surrounds the universe. She felt her numb feet, saw her trembling hands and looked for the escalator to make her way to the kid. Her whole body ached, every muscle, every bone. A glacial air filled her chest and in her eyes there was a new kind of burning. She noticed the deserted halls and remembered her first day on the job, back when she didn't know the fate that hard floor held in store for her. She wanted to be crashed out on her bed, she wanted to escape the nightmare, to smash all the store windows and to be dazzled by a blazing sun.

She eventually found the escalator that would take her down and she told herself, Roxi, keep calm, you'll be with him soon. In the background she heard a sad song and recognised the tune, the one David had been singing to himself, the one that had played in her dream. She remembered every note, the whole chorus and all the verses, and she started singing that dirge as if it were sprouting from her chest. She stepped onto the escalator and started running towards her friend telling herself, Roxi, that's enough, it all ends with you.

How Roxana ran,
so sure, so fleet of foot
step after step
to reach the kid.

She ran like the wind,
ran along an endless course
ran as if an open exit door
awaited her below.

And Roxana kept on running,
they say she's still there,
halfway up that escalator
that never goes down, it keeps on rising.

it keeps on rising, goes the end of the elegy for the suicide victims:

To the continent's tip,
To the blind spot, the lone zone,
Running, rising
Dying with wings,
Falling in mid-song.

Bedwyr Williams

MILITIA

The gallery staff had been locked in the gallery's offices for almost four days when the first of the Militia managed to find a way in. The museum quarter of the city, of which the gallery was a part, hadn't been the focus for any of the groups that had been occupying shops and public spaces with impunity for almost a week, but when they saw the giant anchor outside the keel-shaped maritime museum crashed in through its keel-shaped glass annexe, they knew that the gallery would be next.

They came via the gift shop after peeling back the security shutter. From the recently upgraded security cameras (the old ones had become totally blind after years of staring at bright white walls), the Director could see that the intruders had browsed briefly before they started smashing things up. She shook her head quietly as large shrink-wrapped exhibition catalogues were thrown across the shop, smashing into works for sale on the shelves, sending splinters of ceramic and coloured glass across the floor. Some of the younger-looking Militia started launching craft items upwards towards the ceiling and pretended to run for cover as they came back down. The components of a humorous porcelain tea set in the shapes of breasts, bottoms and genitals were lobbed one by one into the light well of the basement level, where the toilets and cloakrooms were.

The gallery's incredibly heavy (MDF heavy not coin heavy) pyramid-shaped collections box was tipped over on its side and the last six months of coins and the three twenty pound notes they always left in there were pocketed.

The till was yanked from its moorings. The Shop Manager at the Director's side looking at the screen, breathing noisily, could see some of his personal belongings being passed and thrown around.

He saw his small umbrella opened up and destroyed, and the rubber clogs he wore during the day, behind the cast concrete counter, flung somewhere behind the carousels of greetings cards. Finally, an index card system with the details of all the different makers who supplied the shop was tossed into the air.

'Surprise surprise! Now they're looking at the naked pictures in the photography section,' the Shop Assistant said.

'Are they? Are they? We might not agree with anything these people say they stand for, but we should be careful what we mock them about,' the Director cautioned.

The Education Officer was almost certain that they knew one of the Militia. It was someone she had been to school with but wasn't friends with particularly. He was on Facebook and sometimes promoted a small digger hire business.

'He's a big guy,' one of the Technicians said.

'He wasn't big at school, I mean, I don't remember him being big, he says funny things on Facebook sometimes,' the Education Officer said. 'Not ok political stuff I mean.'

She winced as she saw the activity backpacks, hung in a row on the wall for children who visited, being emptied onto the floor and then flung like frisbees towards the accessible toilet.

'Oh, for god's sake what's the point of that, what is the point of that?' she said through her fingers, muffling herself.

As it was changeover in Gallery 2, there were a lot of Technicians around. They had felt pressure from the moment they had barricaded themselves in the gallery over the weekend to step up as the natural defenders of the space.

'I find it so patronising that you see us that way, most of us have our own practices! We're artists not mercenaries, for fuck sake, and we are also scared,' the Head Technician said.

'What about the tools? Could you use them in some way?' a person who had been doing some consultation work at the gallery said.

'A nail gun isn't a gun!' said the Technician with a large beard, his voice rising in pitch.

'A nail gun isn't a gun!' he said again but quietly and slowly.

'Well, can I just say that we all feel safer with you around,' the Director said also in a quiet voice.

'That's great, but we don't feel incredibly safe,' said another Technician who had recently shaved his beard off. He was well-liked in the gallery because of his high level of skill and attention to detail, but, aside from that, the office staff, all on some level, found him cute like a woodland creature. He was unaware of this framing of himself but did sometimes feel infantilised in meetings and some informal work events.

After moving on from the gift shop, it was as if the Militia didn't really know how to navigate the space of the gallery itself.

114

The exhibition, whose run had recently been extended, was by a Peruvian artist who worked with aluminium rods, blocks of plaster and found swatches of fabric. They were 'works that combined tension and a latent fragility', a young man who'd been paid to write about the exhibition wrote. One of the Militia started pushing the works over with one hand as they were relatively light. The springiness of the sculptures meant that they rocked and lolled a little, but as soon as the balance was tipped, and the cubes of plaster hit the concrete floor, they smashed.

The Administrator watching the CCTV started to cry. She was a very valued member of staff, but was not particularly interested in the work exhibited at the gallery, and rarely attended any of the openings or functions apart from the Christmas party, although she often said that she loved the building. 'I love this place, the ladies' loos are in the wrong place, but I bloody love it,' she'd said once.

The Director was surprised to see her react so strongly to the vandalism, which made her feel like she wanted to cry too.

Within an hour of the breach of the security shutter, there were about five hundred people in the gallery, the Shop Assistant was able to estimate this with the sensor near the entrance used to measure footfall.

It seemed as if the blank white walls of the gallery appealed to the Militia, as if they could focus on what they were doing more easily in a context that was neutral architecturally. The rampaging that had gone on in the gift shop initially gave way to a more serious milling around. Some of the Militia put their hands in their pockets and swivelled their heels as they chatted to each other.

The PA system that was used for events and performances had been left in Gallery 3 since an event the previous weekend that had been cancelled at the last minute. The Militia hooked it up and played music from their phones. Like in most galleries, the acoustics were awful, and all the gallery staff could make out were bassy honks and quacks, and the odd vibration of a door or window. 'It's so weird,' the Administrator said, 'it sounds like any other opening.'

Things had taken a more gentile turn, but as the evening passed and alcohol was brought into the building, pockets of raucousness bubbled over. The Director told the rest of the staff that she was going into her office for a moment. She had an afternoon routine that she had been doing for nearly two years. A routine that had actually become a compulsion.

She liked to push her office chair backwards, pacing in reverse towards the bare, polished concrete wall behind her desk. The office chair had a relatively low back and a springy tilt, which allowed her to get right up close to the wall. By performing the manoeuvre slowly, she could dock with the wall so gently she barely made a sound. She liked pressing the nape of her neck against the wall to feel the coolness. It was a subtle chill charge that almost immediately put her in a trance-like state.

Whilst in this position, she could hear sounds from elsewhere in the building. She became plugged into the rumbles and plumbing noises. She was able to relax in such a way that the coolness of the building and the noises transported her out of the building. It never cured her afternoon tiredness as such but rather reshuffled it. She was able to tune into memories of her choosing.

Often she would picture herself as a little child listening to a bath being run for her at her grandparents' house. And it was to this bathroom that she went on this occasion. A bathroom in a room that had once been a bedroom like a lot of bathrooms in older houses. An old deep bath with bulging taps that pointed straight down. A bathroom with black tiles with thin grouting, with a purple toothbrush for her grandfather's dentures in a beaker. Where the coolness would be slowly taken over by steam. There hadn't been a lot of plastic around then, she thought, picturing the denture brush in the beaker. She imagined an owl in the yew tree outside and the smell of bath salts being woken by hot water. After ten minutes or so, she piloted her heavy reverie out of the bathroom and back into the fabric of the building, steering it into the depth of the concrete, thinking for a moment as she went about the ongoing situation at the gallery. She could smell the concrete, the smell she smelled when she came into work early. Each time she went about her afternoon, she felt she was in the walls like a warm fossil person.

'Listen to me,' the concrete said.

The Director could hear the concrete saying it through her whole body.

'I'm not the concrete, I'm not the aggregate. I'm the cement. I am cement; I am a cement product.'

'I understand,' the Director mouthed.

'You're here because of intruders I think,' the cement said.

'Yes, I am.'

'And you want me to persuade them to leave, is that what you want?'

'Yes I do, I do want that,' the Director replied.

'They will be gone in the morning.'

'Thank you,' The Director said.

Back in the galleries some of the Militia were getting frustrated by the flush, fob-operated, handle-less doors. They had a sense that there was more of the building that they hadn't accessed yet. They couldn't barge them, and they couldn't get any purchase around the edge of the doors to pull them open either. The doors had been designed and engineered in such a way that from some angles and in some light, they seemed almost invisible, with only the grubby marks left by the invigilators around the sensors giving them away.

'I mean the whole concept of the development of the building was to kind of disappear the office space behind the walls,' the Assistant Curator said, watching them on the CCTV, 'to be honest I don't think they know we're here.'

'Well, I think that's naïve,' the Technician with the beard replied.

The Director walking back into the room smiled at the rest of the staff. She took a chocolate out of a box that had been brought back from a trip to Qatar by the Senior Curator and said, 'They will be gone in the morning.'

RN
E
N
:
3
O

Crystal
Bennes

A SCIENTIFIC UTOPIA

2018: 16 October, 23:55, Meyrin, Switzerland

I'm in the library at the European Council for Nuclear Research (CERN), sitting at a large desk, my laptop to one side, a pile of books to the other. There's no one else here, although I passed a small group of people drinking and playing board games in the otherwise empty cafeteria on my walk from the onsite hotel through the maze of interconnected buildings to the library. Officially, I have been invited to CERN by two physicists who are attempting to establish a new art-science programme. They both work on the ATLAS experiment, one of four large detectors that sit around the Large Hadron Collider (LHC). Having seen an artwork I completed in 2015, recreating an ATLAS data visualisation as a large stained-glass window, they extended an invitation in the hope that I will create a new work as part of their programme. But I am also here because of my practice-based visual art PhD, which I started a few weeks earlier, looking at feminist critiques of physics.

Today, many physicists (indeed, many scientists) regularly make the surprising claim that science is not political and that politics has no place in science. One aim of my PhD is to challenge such claims by situating the content of physics research, and by extension the sites where it takes place, within their historical, economic and social contexts. The establishment of an institution such as CERN is not, strictly speaking, a purely scientific enterprise, yet it is initiated and carried out by scientists. To successfully realise such a project, scientists must engage in decision making and negotiation, politics and diplomacy. This is why, among other things, the history surrounding the inception of CERN reveals the political nature of science. Hence, my visit to the library.

Although it is nearly midnight, I flip through books and search CERN's online archives for documents from the institution's earliest days. Unlike the library I'm currently sitting in, which is open twenty-four hours a day, the physical archives are accessible only by appointment with the archivist, locked away in the basement behind the sort of door one often sees guarding bank vaults in Hollywood films. Luckily, many archival documents have been digitised and made available online. Just when I think I ought to head back to my room, I discover an unusual letter. The letter reads:

Genève, 15 février 1952

Professor I. Rabi,
Columbia University,
New York, N/Y.

We have just signed the Agreement which constitutes the official birth of the project you fathered at Florence. Mother and child are doing well, and the Doctors send you their greetings.

The 'we' in this letter comprises the twenty-two attendees of the very first meeting of CERN's provisional Council. Professor I. Rabi, to whom the letter is addressed, is Isidor Rabi, an American theoretical physicist often referred to as the 'father of CERN'. The letter's reference to Florence is a nod to Rabi's pitch for regional European laboratories following the Second World War, which provided the impetus for CERN, at a UNESCO meeting in Florence in June 1950. Rabi framed the letter and hung it on the wall of his home office.

1952: 6 October, Amsterdam, The Netherlands

Today marks the third day of the third CERN Council meeting, when the location for the new laboratory will finally be decided. Four governments have made proposals to host: the Danes have offered Copenhagen; the Dutch, Arnhem; the French suggested Longjumeau, just outside Paris; and the Swiss proposed Geneva. Yesterday, all meeting delegates visited nearby Arnhem for a site inspection. Now the debate begins in earnest. Each of the four representatives has been briefed by their respective officials to put forward persuasive arguments in favour of locating the laboratory in their country. The competition is intense. The scientific prestige of being selected would be a boon, but all are aware that the real prize will be financial gain, courtesy of an abundance of industrial contracts and technological spin-offs.

The French offer a site in the neighbourhood of Paris, together with the necessary facilities for housing staff. The Dutch offer thirty-four hectares and the peace and quiet necessary for strenuous intellectual endeavours. The Danes offer a suitable area of about 200,000 square meters situated between a public park and the harbour. The Swiss offer thirty hectares and diplomatic privileges similar to those granted to other inter-governmental organisations. But most importantly, the Swiss offer neutrality, something no other government can provide.

Except for the Danes, there is no support for Copenhagen. Niels Bohr is already too dominant in physics. No one wants him to become even more powerful. Some are tempted by Paris. It is conveniently located. The culture is good. As is the food. But surely, the French government would not be able to resist interfering. No to France, then. Better to locate CERN in a small country, one less likely to meddle. That leaves Arnhem and Geneva. Debate intensifies. Deep-seated political alliances come into play. Italy unwaveringly supports Switzerland. Given that Paris is no longer in contention, the French, too, support Geneva. Better a neighbour, they reason, with whom they share a language and a culture than the Netherlands. Realising that the French will never agree to Arnhem, the Dutch withdraw their proposed site from consideration. They grasp that without the French the entire project might never happen. Better to have CERN in Geneva than to have no CERN at all. With all other options eliminated, the Council decides unanimously in favour of Geneva.

2020: 19 June, 12:00, Edinburgh, United Kingdom

In normal circumstances, meetings of CERN's governing body are held in the large, domed auditorium within the campus's main building. But with the Covid-19 pandemic – non-essential shops still have not reopened where I live in Edinburgh and most people continue to work from home – the 199th Council meeting is being held via Zoom. Delegates from the twenty-three current member states have logged on from all over Europe. Some are in casual clothes in their home offices, bookshelves on display; others are dressed in suits and ties in their labs or university offices. The session's agenda includes a recap of the 2019 annual progress and financial reports, but the main item is a vote on a resolution. This resolution comprises the 2020 update of the European Strategy for Particle Physics which will set the trajectory of the field for the next twenty years, including plans for the Future Circular Collider (FCC), the successor to the LHC.

Whether by nature or by design, physicists tend to be forward-looking. In many cases, even before a new experiment is operational, its kinks not fully ironed out, the next generation iterations will have already been in discussion. Sometimes it feels as if experimental physics were a never-ending Ponzi scheme. Although the LHC has been operational since 2008, discussions around what comes next have been taking place long before this Council meeting: publicly, since 2013; privately, for a lot longer.

On Zoom, the current FCC plans are summarised in a Strategy Statements slideshow, delivered in comic sans, CERN's unofficial-official font. The plans entail the building of the FCC, projected to be four times the size of the LHC, in stages until around the 2050s, when it would be operating with an energy around six times higher than the LHC's maximum capability. And while the vast majority of experimental physicists who work at CERN or for its partner institutions are fully in favour of the FCC, the project has become increasingly controversial. The chief complaint largely stems from the FCC's projected cost of twenty-one billion euros, all of which must be paid for by the governments of CERN's member states. As one of the FCC's most vocal critics, theoretical physicist Sabine Hossenfelder, recently argued in *Scientific American*, 'Building larger particle colliders has run its course. It has today little scientific return on investment, and at the same time almost no societal relevance.' Hossenfelder wonders why such funds are not diverted, for example, to the pressing issues of climate change research. These views make Hossenfelder a deeply unpopular figure at CERN. Unsurprisingly, the controversy passes unmentioned in the Strategy Statements presentation.

Following the general overview, the Council's chair calls on delegates from each of the member states in alphabetical order and asks whether or not they will adopt the resolution. All states adopt the resolution. The vote feels like a formality. Each delegate, as part of their response, makes a brief speech expressing their state's belief in both the importance of the strategy and implementing it to maintain Europe's position as the world leader in particle physics. From a timber-clad room which could be either an office within a university or a garden shed, the delegate from Denmark responds: 'We think it's a visionary strategy that has all the components necessary to ensure a vibrant future for European high energy physics, including a powerful and innovative technological development programme, thus serving intellectual and technological goals as well as concrete developments that will benefit society at large.'

Why is it, I wonder, that particle physicists only seem to make sweeping claims about the benefits of their research to 'society at large' when they are trying to raise funds for their increasingly expensive experiments. Most of the rest of the time, they are content, proud even, to speak about physics as the science of 'pure' rather than 'applied' research.

1953: 27-28 June, Geneva, Switzerland

Somehow, word had got out. A nuclear physics research facility is to be constructed in Geneva. Who authorised the decision? Will the facility produce military weapons? What about possible health risks to Genevan citizens? Would not the existence of such a facility pose too great a risk to Switzerland's cherished cultural and political identity as a neutral state?

Following an impassioned campaign spearheaded by the local Communist Party opposing the location of a nuclear physics research facility in Geneva, enough signatures are collected to force a public vote on the issue. The Swiss Council of States sets dates for a referendum: the weekend of 27 and 28 June 1953. The vote will be whether or not 'to prohibit the establishment of an international institute for nuclear physics in the canton of Geneva'.

The referendum takes place.

Votes are tallied.

16,528 against prohibition of CERN and 7,332 in favour.

2020: 29 April, 12:43, Edinburgh, United Kingdom

From my desk at home, I search the digitised archives of the *Journal de Genève* for articles about the Communist Party's campaign against building CERN in Switzerland. In the secondary sources, the precise reasons for their disapproval are often unclear. There is also confusion about the result of the vote.

I discover a number of interesting articles, including opinion pieces expressing both support and condemnation. Eventually, I find a newspaper notice announcing the dates of the CERN referendum vote. Above that notice, another announcement immediately catches my eye. It publicises a meeting of the Action Committee for Female Suffrage to be held in Geneva on Friday 5 June 1953. How curious, I think. Why a rally on female suffrage in the early 1950s? Surely, in 1953, women had the right to vote in Switzerland? A quick check, however, reveals that it was not until 1960 that women obtained the right to vote in local elections in Geneva. And it was not until 1971 that women finally won the vote in Swiss national elections – particularly surprising when compared to its nearest neighbours, with Germany and Austria granting the right in 1918 and France and Italy in 1945.

I look again at the dates, then at the voting figures from the 1953 referendum, before realising that of the 23,860 total votes cast to determine the fate of CERN's presence in Switzerland, not a single one was cast by a woman. No mother, sister or daughter in Switzerland had a legal say on locating CERN in Geneva. I recall the letter written to Isidor Rabi by the institution's founding 'doctors' back in 1952, in which CERN is conceptualised as the 'mother and child [who] are doing well'. Women have been excluded from CERN's creation at every stage – they could not vote for or against its presence in their country, they did not serve on its Council – yet the men who dreamt up its very existence gendered it female, maternal even.

2020: 19 February, 14:30, Meyrin, Switzerland

I'm back at CERN. I had forgotten how unattractive it is. The low winter light is wonderful, though, as I stand on a small hill near the antimatter factory, admiring the view of the Alps on one side and the Jura on the other.

Apart from its overwhelming shabbiness, the most irritating aspect of CERN is the extent to which it feels designed for cars. Looking at a satellite view of the site, it is evident that almost as much space has been given over to parking as to buildings. With my medium-format camera and a heavy tripod slung over my shoulder, I walk the entire length of the site on a weekday afternoon and meet no one else on foot. Sunshine glints off the corrugated metal panels that clad most buildings. One of CERN's quirkier habits is to name buildings not by description or function, as you might find on a university campus, but simply by number. Although immensely frustrating for newcomers to navigate, the mysterious anonymity of numbered buildings is catnip to those of us nosy by nature. What is hidden within building 65, I wonder as I skirt its perimeter. I spend entire days of my visit, unescorted and unaccompanied, trying my ID card on doors of buildings I am probably not supposed to enter. They open surprisingly often.

Non-scientific visitors are frequently astonished by the distinct lack of aesthetic interest at CERN. How can it be that such enormous budgets do not buy more beautiful buildings? In general, investment in architecture is not, and never has been, a foremost concern at CERN. From its inception, spending priorities have essentially boiled down to all science, all of the time. Given the vast amounts of money required to build particle accelerators and their experimental detectors, physicists already operate in a highly competitive funding environment – if there is not enough money for research, what scientist would support funding for extraneous luxuries such as architecture? That said, CERN's public relations department has lately changed its opinion as to the value of grand architectural gestures in the never-ending quest to garner broader public support and increased financial contributions from member states. In 2019, after years of architectural neglect, CERN announced plans for a new 'iconic' building to house an education and outreach centre designed by Renzo Piano. In line with its budget priorities, however, the new building will not actually be paid for by CERN, but by private donations. Inspired apparently by the 'fragmentation and curiosity intrinsic to the nature of the CERN site and buildings', the building's design is essentially a series of five interconnected pavilions, three boxy and two tubular, spanning the large, busy road leading into central Geneva. This orientation to the road is deliberate. With everything else fenced off behind security checkpoints for authorised visitors only, the road is essentially the only public space at CERN. Piano's design appears generous while maintaining this strict boundary between public and private space.

1955: 5 September, New York City, United States

When mankind got electricity and steam, factories sprang up, and residential sections were thrown around them without planning. That's what we must avoid in the atomic age. The architect should be Number One.

So declares Rudolf Steiger, the architect hired by CERN's first Council to design the site masterplan and all technical and administrative buildings. He is being interviewed by a journalist from *Time* magazine for an upcoming profile. It has been two years since construction began on site in Geneva. The journalist ponders how best to describe Steiger, who he has been told is Switzerland's top architect. Perhaps 'outspoken'. He settles on 'a blunt bundle of energy' and makes a note to include it in the article.

Although Steiger is a partner in Haefeli Moser Steiger, an important Swiss firm, he also runs a practice under his own name. When CERN calls to offer the commission, Steiger is preoccupied with designing a new hospital in Zurich: 'I designed everything, down to the laundry truck. Every purchase order, no matter how small, passed my desk,' he tells the *Time* journalist. Steiger hands over the bulk of the CERN project to his son Peter, only twenty-one, with no built work to his name. Peter has recently returned from working with Frank Lloyd Wright in Arizona with a passion for urban planning.

Prior to commencing design work on CERN, Steiger father and son tour atomic research laboratories in the US. Among other sites, they visit Brookhaven in New York and Oak Ridge National Laboratories in Tennessee. Rudolf Steiger is unimpressed. He thinks the US labs look like gold miners' settlements, planned and built in stages, with no overall design. Steiger is vehemently opposed to this way of what he calls 'building by committee'. To his mind, there is no reason why technical requirements should 'degenerate architecture'. But Steiger has not encountered a client quite like CERN before. This is not comparable to his recently-completed Zurich hospital where, when one of the surgeons objected to what he called Steiger's unorthodox arrangement of the operating rooms, the architect suggested that the surgeon might be happier working elsewhere. CERN has functional requirements which Steiger must accommodate. For the technical and scientific buildings in particular, a number of important practical concerns take precedence over aesthetics. Sun and wind directions must be taken into careful consideration. Where Steiger wants a concentrated cluster of buildings to give a campus-like feel, CERN's physicists caution that unknowns around potential radiation emissions mean it will be preferable to space them apart. The Steigers eventually decide on a small but coherent complex of administrative buildings, workshops and laboratories, together with buildings housing CERN's first particle accelerators. In the final plan, laboratories will orient north-south as per the direction of the wind, the largest lab buildings will be situated to the west and the smaller labs and offices to the east. The heart of the campus will be CERN's Main Building, home to the library, restaurant and auditorium, and one of the few instances in which Steiger has been aesthetically triumphant. The grand Main Building entrance will open onto a monumental staircase, with geometric mosaic floor tiles designed by his artist friend, and statuesque mushroom pillars inspired by Peter's time working with Lloyd Wright.

2020: 19 February, 11:45, Cessy, France

Last time I was at CERN, the proton beam was continuously operational for the entirety of my stay so I was never able to visit any of the underground detectors. On this visit, however, the beam is off because of a planned long-term shutdown, and detector visits are back on. In Cessy, about a half-hour drive away from the main campus near Geneva, I admire the spectacle of a 14,000-tonne extremely high-resolution camera situated a hundred metres belowground. This is the Compact Muon Solenoid (CMS) detector, one of four experiments situated along the 26.7-kilometre circumference of the LHC ring. Although it is interesting to visit in person, there is something faintly disappointing about the experience. Visitors are restricted to access platforms and walkways so the available perspective of the detector is the same one I have seen before in hundreds of photographs. I am standing in front of the detector, yet I am looking at an image. How uncanny to experience a thing that seems almost no different from its representation.

1998: 10 July, Cessy, France

Construction crews are preparing the site for the CMS detector cavern in a neighbouring field. They hit a snag. Beneath the grass and soil lies a fourth-century Roman villa. Work halts for six months while an archaeological team excavates and catalogues the site. The archaeologists finish their work and a decision is made: the villa will be carefully covered up and reburied so that detector construction can proceed as planned.

2020: 19 February, 12:25, Cessy, France

The physicist accompanying me around CMS makes a throw-away quip about the fact that the detector was born, lived and will almost certainly die in this underground cavern. It makes for a striking parallel with the fate of the nearby Roman villa. Because it was so expensive, time-consuming and difficult to install the CMS detector in its current location, it's a near certainty that the cavern – detector and all – will simply be backfilled with concrete when the LHC eventually shuts down. Useful scraps will be reclaimed, of course, but it would cost an enormous amount of money to retrieve what will by then be an obsolete particle physics detector, and no scientific committee would approve such a use of funds. Instead, CMS will simply be concealed, as if it had never been there in the first place.

Postscript: Excavating CERN in 4041

Unlike the robust stone and mortar of medieval cathedrals, most of CERN was never built to last. That even some of the original structures designed by Steiger have survived more than fifty years is surprising. It seems impossible to imagine that in the far distant future anything at CERN as it stands today would remain. Yet future ruin, though rarely acknowledged by those working in the field, is almost integral to the practice of experimental physics. Site buildings are often cobbled together on miniscule budgets. Even early iterations of detectors are often patched together from whatever materials can be salvaged from the wreckage of previous experiments. And every experiment has a limited life span, making it all the more remarkable that end-of-life planning (decommissioning, recycling, disposing, etc.) plays almost no part in the initial design discussions or reports. Physicists think about future experiments, but not about the future repercussions of those experiments.

And although concrete will perhaps make it more difficult for future archaeologists to excavate CERN's relics than if its detectors were merely backfilled with sand and soil, it is not impossible to imagine someone digging up part of the CMS detector 2,000 years from now and puzzling over its function. When the Roman villa was discovered in the late 1990s, despite a timespan of more than 1,500 years, it was not beyond the realm of possibility for archaeologists to piece together the finds and draw conclusions about how people lived, perhaps even what they believed in. But for those who dig up CERN's concrete-covered caverns in the far distant future, it is difficult to imagine what kind of world they might dream up based on enormous pieces of decomposing particle detectors or what conclusions they might draw about the civilisation that created them in the first place.

OF TIME

&

Jodie Azhar

MECHANICS

OXYTOCIN

Game developer Jodie Azhar is the founder and CEO of Teazelcat Games, a studio focused on story-driven games, where she is directing their first title. We interviewed her for the first time in February 2020 at the Whitechapel Gallery – then we talked about time mechanics, digital space and virtual reality. That conversation ignited our interest in games, and particularly the worlds their developers create for players to enter and 'inhabit', as well as the possibilities of interactive storytelling where the narrative shifts in response to the actions of the player. We are continuing that conversation here, looking at how we can move between pixels and ink, and exploring the ever-expanding medium of video games that has a lot more to offer than an escape into a parallel universe.

Justinien Tribillon [JT], Jodie Azhar [JA]

JT   Perhaps we could start at the beginning: what is a video game?

JA   It's quite hard to define exactly what a video game is. The key element that makes something a video game is the digital experience of playing, interacting, as opposed to, say, the passive experience of watching a film. In a video game you have to think. The thinking might just be about how to progress the story, or it might be about making decisions on your next steps in the game, on what your player does, or it could be a puzzle game experience which requires some playfulness.

JT   And how did you find yourself developing games?

JA   When I went to university, I studied computer programming, graphics and 3D animation. I really enjoyed the creative subjects, but I also have a very technical mind. I think a lot of game developers either sway very heavily towards the creative or the technical side. I wanted to do both. My thinking then was that I'd go into film and feature animation, that I'd end up doing something like Disney or Pixar films, but while I was studying, I realised that the skills that I was developing were applicable to video game development, which is all about the marriage of creativity and technology. When I graduated, I found myself in a job as a video game animator, and I did that for a year and then went into technical animation and technical art, marrying programming and art. I spent half of my career working on *Total War* (developed by Creative Assembly), a strategy game franchise. And now I work more on independent games with a strong narrative focus.

JT What game are you developing now?

JA I've spent most of my career working on games centred around combat. It is a very common game mechanic because, when there is conflict, it's very easy to see where the gameplay lies. There is a mix of conflict and cooperation between you and other players, or with the artificial intelligence in the game. Yet, I don't feel we explore enough in these kinds of games. We barely touch on other ideas of cooperation, or the positive effects of making friends, of developing relationships in video games.

 The reason for this is partly because those other aspects are difficult to quantify. When you defeat a given number of enemies, in a classic combat game, you can say, 'I'm really powerful because of my numbers. My levels have gone up.' You can see a numeric increase. It's harder to approach other feelings in the same way: feelings such as being nice to another player in a game or another human in real life. You can say you feel good, but you can't see your *levels of friendship* necessarily going up.

 I want to explore these other possibilities of creating relationships in games. That's why I'm currently making a narrative game where you can choose how to interact with other characters. You can become friends with them or, equally, you can choose to be antagonistic. And rather than having a numeric value, actions in the game reflect whether they like you or not in return. And you, as a player and a human being, should feel progress by developing your relationships with the games' characters in the way you see fit.

 I really want to explore this approach to gaming because I think combat games don't appeal to a large part of the population.

So many people now play video games and, a lot of the time, they don't quite realise it because the game might be an app on their phone. They might not even consider themselves as a gamer, because they do not play on a console, but actually they spend a good hour a day playing, whether it's during their commute or just killing time sitting on the sofa.

The gender balance for video game players is almost equal. And actually one of the biggest demographics is women over the age of forty. When you consider all the popular games that appeal primarily to a younger male audience, you realise there's a significant demographic group who want video game experiences but aren't looking for fighting games. And one of those people is my mum. I grew up playing video games with her. She loves point and click adventures, games with a story or a puzzle-solving element, but she doesn't want anything where she has to have fast reaction time or has to fight. That's why I keep her in mind when I'm developing my game: will she understand how to play this game?; will she understand how to progress?; will she enjoy the exploration?

JT   How do you write a script for a video game? How do you conceive it?

JA   This depends on the type of game you're making. If you're making a game that, time-wise, goes from point A to point B, with events happening in a linear fashion throughout, you can essentially write it in the same way you'd write a film script. And then it's up to you, as a narrative designer or a writer, to see what works best. Does it make sense to start writing the beginning and the end before filling in the major events that happen in the middle? Or you might prefer to write it in a linear fashion, from the beginning through the middle to the end.

The game I'm working on at the moment is very much choice-based. Therefore, one of the issues I have is that depending on what you, the player, choose to do, you will get different options, and different characters will treat you differently. One of the challenges is that if you antagonise a character at a certain point in game-time, you will essentially cut yourself off from any future events where you could have a pleasant relationship. This is because it would seem really unnatural for you to go and kick someone before suddenly turning around and saying: 'Oh, do you want to go out for a picnic?'

That's why I have to plot the major story points the character will go through and then find a natural way, through different pathways, of reaching those story points. Otherwise, there could be different sequences of events that many players won't even see, because they depend on their previous engagement with other characters.

To write I use an open-source software called Twine, which is essentially a digital version of sticky notes. You write all your events as a script sequence, and then you can connect how one event leads to another, allowing you to see the pathways through the game.

JT How do you approach narrative in relation to interaction? Are you the mastermind of your game, or do you design it so the game's story has a life of its own, outside of your control?

JA I think that one of the really exciting things with technological knowledge is that it's possible to create a game which is completely reactionary, where you, as a player, can go down a path that the developer no longer has complete control over. It takes a lot of time to get the technology right for that to work because, obviously, the more control you have as a creator, the more you can tailor the experience, and tailor the exact story of the player's character, or the people in your game's world.

Yet for creative people who want to tell a specific story, it makes sense to limit the amount of choice that a player has. Instead, the game can be about giving players the illusion of choice. Players will still need to make decisions, but, ultimately, they won't be world-changing in the game. For instance, this might be about allowing the player to unlock a certain part of the story – some players might get different experiences when accessing this, but the core story will remain the same. Whereas I think if you want to go down the route where everything the player does in the game has an impact, then you have to give up some control as a creator and focus more on the technology.

JT Time is a tool in the narrative, you can rewind, play forward, be reborn and start again, your action might trigger the story to progress, etc. How do you integrate that in your game narrative?

JA There are so many ways you can use time in video games because it doesn't require constant updating of the narrative as it would in a film. When you press play, a movie will play at exactly the pace that the director and the editor have put it together. But a game relies on the player's input. If the player doesn't input, the story won't progress. But as a game developer, you could still make elements of the game progress. For instance, if the player just stands there, game-time might still progress with non-playable characters carrying on doing what they're doing. Eventually, they could lock the player out of different parts of the story.

It's a really interesting and powerful puzzle-solving mechanic. What if two weeks ago, when you started the game, there was a ladder in the room. You're currently locked in this room, and there's a window really high up, and you've got no way of getting out, but you've got this mechanic where you can move forward and backward in time. If you go back in time, grab a ladder and bring it forward, then you can climb up and reach the window.

One of the things that isn't thought enough about by developers, in my opinion, is that you never know when players are going to play the game. With a film, you traditionally sit down and watch the entire story in one sitting. The viewing happens within a short enough period of time for you to remember who all the characters are and what's going on. As a game player, you don't necessarily know if they're going to finish the whole game in one sitting. With a big game that has sixty hours of story and side quests, you might not remember what you were doing in the game last week or last month, or two months ago, when you started the game. And the game developer might not know in what order you will talk to different characters, or in what order you will ask questions. Players have to remember all the events that happen in the game and all the different characters they meet. Also, one day of the player's time could cover months or years in game-time.

I don't think anyone wrote down the rules of time mechanics for games. It's not something you're taught at school. You pick it up by playing video games and inventing new ones.

JT   You mentioned the intricate relationship between numbers and progress in games: the measured achievements. There are some really interesting parallels with urban planning that is constantly trying to quantify everything: code its progress. Boxes need to be ticked. As a creative, whose ambition is to develop a game that focuses on subtle feelings, how do you negotiate that tension between *qualitative* and *quantitative*, as we would say in social sciences?

JA   I like to look at the technical aspect as a way of maximising creativity. I think it can spawn some really interesting ideas because you've got to solve problems, for instance: how do you make your creative vision run on particular hardware? In the past ten years, mobile games skyrocketed in popularity. Before that games were mainly played in the arcades, on consoles or PCs. You created your video game to run on a particular console or you assumed that the player's PC is going to be powerful enough for the game. Phones are a lot more limited. You have to design your game for that environment, for instance, when it comes to the level of details being rendered on screen. I actually enjoy the limitations inherent to the development. You can't just constantly ask yourself: 'What's the upper limit of what I can do?' Because you could start making a game that would take three years to develop and in that time technology would have progressed. You could end up being continually on this cycle, waiting for the next technology to be made available.

When you invited me to be part of the public programme at the Whitechapel Gallery in 2020, one of the things that you inspired me to think about was the question of designing space for different people who would have different investment in it. If you're a property developer, you want to maximize that space by, say, fitting in more housing units on a plot of land. This is an example of a numerical approach to the question of space. But when you think about who the users will be and how they're going to use the space, then something that might, in terms of numbers, feel wasteful such as adding green space or creating curved walls that might feel more friendly, more natural, might contribute to people's productivity. If you are designing an office space, then you won't necessarily want to cut it up into cubicles where you can maximize the number of employees. Instead, you might want breakout areas, you might want space where there are plants and natural light. This kind of space is going to feed into the well-being of those working there.

I've already touched on video games' relationship to numerical ways of quantifying achievement, particularly in combat games. With clear numbers, it's very easy to say: 'Okay, if I fight 10 enemies, I'll go up to the next level. If I do this, I'll gain 1000 experiences. That's how I'll level up.' The player gets a nice rush of adrenaline and endorphins. It's easy to focus on adrenaline, but there are other chemicals that make us feel good, such as oxytocin. Oxytocin is created when we protect others, when we make friends. You get a different reward from being kind to a person than you do from winning something or defeating an enemy. In the same way that making green spaces or breakout areas in a physical architectural space is rewarding to people and might improve productivity, making people feel good inside a video game without focusing on numerical achievements that are linked to adrenaline might be equally rewarding in a different way.

JT   This makes me think that video games are all about manipulation of the players' most intimate emotions. Is that what it's about?

JA   I don't think we as game designers try to hide the manipulation aspect, but it has to feel natural. This works in a very similar way in films. If you want people to feel a strong emotion in response to a story, you need to make the viewer, or the player, invested in it. If you kill a character in the middle of a film, but you haven't built the relationship between the viewer and that character, that person can die without much emotional impact. Alternatively, if you get the viewer, or player, invested in who that character is, then their death will be experienced as a loss. In video games, characters are completely digital, they are not even an actor, but you can still get that exact same emotional response.

JT   And the interactive nature of games is probably increasing that feeling. Do you think that video games, like photography or writing or theatre, are becoming an art medium in their own right? The aesthetics and tropes of video games are everywhere now.

JA   I believe we're going to see more products that cross over between different realms or industries. Interactive, branching narratives are becoming more and more common in TV series, theatre, as well as video games of course. You can have more of an interactive experience as an audience participant in a physical sphere. For a game developer, it is difficult to draw a line that says: 'This is a video game, and this is something else.' And it's almost not up to us to decide where that line is drawn. It might be only possible to define it through the natural progression of language, and people who use interactivity as a medium that defies categories. We've started raising the question of what interactive experiences count as video games on the BAFTA games committee where I sit. That's absolutely brilliant. But then, you get into debates about what a video game is or what is not, what TV is, what craft is, what film is, etc. In any case, this leads to different types of creative people collaborating together, and for me, as a creator, that's very exciting.

JT   We have to ask before concluding this interview, considering our topic, any thoughts on city-builder games?

JA   I find them really interesting because of their relationship to time and simulation. You can observe game-time moving forward in the simulation without the players' input. It acts almost as a research project where players might enjoy seeing a city they've built live on, being left alone, so to speak. What will each of these buildings do if you just leave it alone? And how will they interact with each other? Simulations are economies in their own right, and they depend on the rules the developer sets for the game.

Meghana Bisineer

Interview with animation artist

IN BETWEEN

FRAMES

Meghana Bisineer is an Indian-born artist, filmmaker and educator who lives and works in London, UK, and Oakland, California. Animation, game design and puppetry have been recurring topics of curiosity for us throughout the course of this project. We were eager to exchange ideas with Meghana on her artistic practice, her understanding of time, her relationship to architecture, and what home means to her, both as a place and a state of mind.

Justinien Tribillon [JT], Meghana Bisineer [MB], Marta Michalowska [MM]

JT   Let's start with the basics: what is animation? And how did you become an artist working with animation?

MB   Animating is bringing something to life. You can do that through a series of sequential drawings or using other techniques and materials. You are taking movement and breaking it down into time, and then breaking the time down into a sequence of images. When our eye is looking at a series of stills projected in front of us at a certain speed, the eye and the brain are stitching up these images to create an illusion of movement. This is called the persistence of vision, which makes this magic possible.

After school I did a foundation in fine art in Bangalore, India. I thought I was going to be a painter or a visual artist. And then I went to a design school, the National Institute of Design. This is where I found out about animation.

I love drawing, and I love telling stories. Animation brings both of these aspects together. That's why I went into animation. The animation at the National Institute of Design was mostly traditional, both in form and content. We worked with character-led narratives. We were trained to be filmmakers, and make independent films from start to end. This was in India, in a design school in the nineties, where we had to justify all the stories that we wanted to tell.

My interest in animation also had a lot to do with growing up in India, with mythology, which, since then, has come into my work in so many ways. When I was growing up, I couldn't tell what was

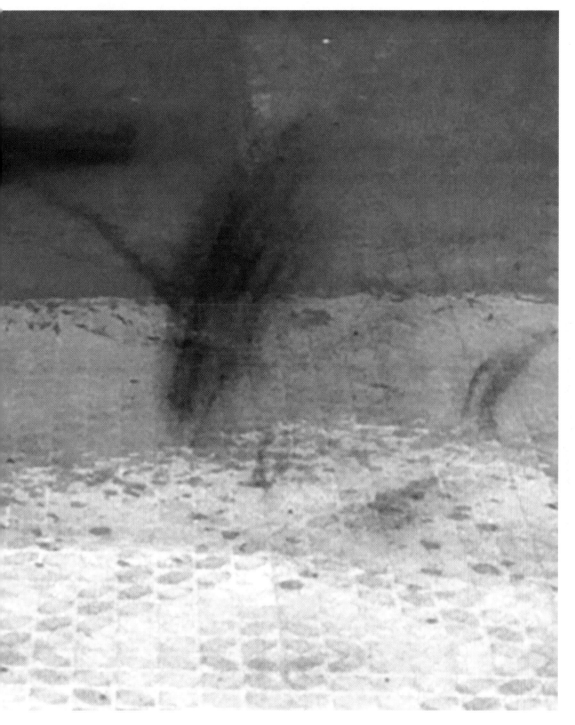

Dust, Meghana Bisineer, 2020

historical and what was mythological, because in everyday life these two overlapped. There was a similar reverence for gods as there was for historical figures, or contemporary ones, all celebrated in that same way. Storytelling, taking the mundane and making it big, making it magnanimous – all that comes from mythology.

I worked in India for some time, but there wasn't really an opportunity to nurture independent filmmaking, and I was really hungry to find out what more was out there in the world. I really loved it, but I felt like I needed to push more to see what else I could do. I got a scholarship to come to London to do my Masters at the Royal College of Art. That's when the whole world of animation as an art form really opened up for me.

There is a lot about animation that I find fascinating, that I think I've just absorbed into my system, that I can't let go of. When you put images together, sequentially, and play them back, you see movement, you see the drawings, but you also see what happens in between these drawings. Animation is not just what is in the frames but what happens in between the frames. It's also a way of thinking, and a way of approaching the world. That's how I see the world.

MM I feel your work is about accumulation, a layering of time: about watching a very slow process unfolding in a time lapse. This process – that in your practice is very much about the decay and ruination of the paper on which you're drawing – seems to be about making time explicit by revealing the accumulation of temporal layers.

MB Yes, absolutely. The materials that are working with me in the studio are also my collaborators: natural light or charcoal or paper or water. I find it increasingly hard as I get older to separate my practice from my life. It is like life, it is life itself. You can't erase the past. Time is layered. We are an accumulation of everything that has been, and who I am in this moment is the result of this – a constantly changing ongoingness. When I'm drawing, I'm drawing in quite a ritualistic way, over the same surface, over an extended period of time. Time is embedded in the work in a very physical way. You see the paper wearing down, or you see the wall accumulating the marks over time. At any point, if you pause at any frame of the animation, it is not just *that* drawing you are looking at, but layers and layers of drawings that have come before, that have been erased and that have been added to, but without which you cannot get to the present.

I'd like to consider the aspect of time in mythology, for example. Time is non-linear and multi-dimensional. More importantly, time is beyond one's current life-span. You are accumulating, and you have the possibility of moving in multiple dimensions – rather than only forward.

Animation allows me to play with time in quite a cosmic way. You can take one moment and really expand it. But you can also take five days and turn them into one second. And that elasticity of time is amazing and fascinating. For instance, when I turned my London studio into a camera obscura, I was slowing time down. I was taking very long exposures of the exterior landscape being projected on the interior of the studio and onto myself, and, through that process, I was slowing time, expanding it. Something was happening between the landscape, myself and the captured image. I was collaborating with all these outside forces which made the work. This process was about giving up control – letting go – as well as being aware and attentive. In a way, it was a dance.

JT   The first element that seems to define animation is that Frankenstein-like act of bringing something to life. This must be a different way to see space and time, because to make a two-minute animated film, it takes days and days and days of work...

MB   Months, and hours every day. And then you just have this two-minute film.

MM   That has a cosmic quality as well.

MB Repetition. This is all about the repetition of time, to which you add natural light and the natural passing of time. When I talk to my students who are just starting out in animation I ask, 'What's most exciting for you?' And they go, 'I feel like God, I'm creating this whole universe, I can do whatever I want, I can control everything.' Yet I, on the other hand, feel like my whole practice has been about letting go of control and really seeing how much I can step back. It's about starting something off, like planting some seeds, and then stepping back, or feeling like an in-between, like a medium. I'm another tool in the collaboration with everything that's going on and try not to control it as much: let the work take its own form.

JT It's fairly healthy that your students admit to that, because, usually, in architecture or urban planning schools they all want to be God, but will never say it out loud. It's not acceptable anymore.

MM I didn't realise that there is such a similarity between the practice of architecture and the practice of animation through creating a universe and wishing to preside over it.

JT Mythologies keep coming back in our discussion. Yet when we consider your work, *Dust* for instance, it's very intimate. It is set in your parents' home. Spaces of intimacy are really present in your work. How do you articulate this?

MB I feel there is timelessness to mythologies, and the reason we are drawn to them is because we can all see ourselves in them, but with a sense of awe and magnification. Then there is the mundane as well: the little nuances. Mythologies are also very much about inner conflicts – the characters going through their inner conflicts – and these play out in a very dramatic way. And to an extent, I can see this happening when I'm working with spaces. It is also a very intimate conversation with place, not just with the physicality of it but with all the unseen energies that places hold. With *Dust*,

Dust, Meghana Bisineer, 2020

Let me not be mad, Meghana Bisineer, 2016

I was working on the terrace of my parents' home, the home where I was born in Bangalore.

Intimacy is an overlapping aspect of my work, the desire to connect with place, or the inability to connect, and having an exchange that either draws me in or pushes me away. And finding home: what does home mean? When I'm having those conversations with the place, it is very much about having those conversations with the self.

I was making *Dust* at the beginning of the pandemic in India, when millions of people, who in the UK would be called *key workers* – the labourers, the street cleaners – were just left stranded. Everything shut down, and they had no option but to start walking for miles over days to get back to their homes and villages. They became completely disposable, in a sense, but they are the ones that keep the whole country going at its very basic level. The song that you hear in *Dust* is an old Kannada folk song. It's a work song, it is about death, but sung while toiling to give energy. It carries in its spirit an ongoingness of life, and a certain futility of it too. The song is about a soul crying out to her sisters while looking down at her own cremation. She is witnessing her own last rites with a feeling of violation and laments as her sari and blouse are removed from her body.

The film is formed around rituals of cleansing and cleaning: a lot of sweeping, washing and layering of mud. Traditionally, that's how the outside of houses is cleansed in India. I built the bamboo structure featured in the film as a symbol of home, as well as a symbol of the female body. I was reflecting on all these aspects, and the position of women in society, as I was just sweeping and washing the floor, layering mud and recording these actions over time.

MM I sometimes think about your work as being inside out, where you project your internal landscape.

MB Yes, absolutely. Just like throwing everything that's inside onto the outside, watching it emerge and then cleaning up after myself.

The Stone, Meghana Bisineer, 2020

Shifting Ground, Meghana Bisineer, 2012

MM   Would you like to talk a little bit more about this idea of constructing, in a way, through time, and through drawing, of a representation not only of an architecture of a place, but also an architecture of intimate elements that holds it together from the inside?

MB   Perhaps I could answer this question through the film *The Stone*, which I made as soon as I arrived in the UK during the first lockdown in spring 2020. I was on sabbatical in Germany when everywhere started shutting down, so I found myself back in London, my old home city. It was a time when I felt rootless. The film happened through an intention to set out a personal ritual to find a rooted space within myself, or come home within the self. I approached the making of this film as a ritual of drawing the same stone every day, over a period of time, and seeing how it changed. Then I filmed the drawings, which were made on semi-transparent tracing paper, on the windows of my friends' homes, where I was staying when I didn't have my own home.

The physicality of the world around is always present in the work. But for me, the stone itself represents an inner world that is alive and pulsating. It is a point of meditation, a point of focus, enabling the possibility to find home, to land.

I didn't realise this at the time of making it, but I grew up meditating on a stone. The community that I come from in India are called the Lingayats. We are not a caste. It started in the twelfth century as a social movement against the caste system, and against all kinds of divisions and barriers. We don't worship idols. The only text we have is poetry written by Basavanna, the person who started this social movement. We have a black stone called the Linga, and that's the only practice: meditating on a stone. When I got to London, I just picked up a stone and decided to draw it. This was going to be my ritual, my meditation, this was going to bring me home, and this was going to give me some sense of stability.

JT I need to add that architecture feels very present in your work. You drew on the window of the estate where you lived in London, you drew on the windows of the Royal Festival Hall with the National Theatre in the background. We have talked about your childhood home in Bangalore. How do you engage with architecture through your practice?

MB I don't see architecture merely as a canvas or a background. I think it is about intimacy: the relationship that I have with spaces. I tend to spend a lot of time in spaces where the works are made. I'm often exploring what that relationship with a particular place and space is, and how it plays out in the minute marks or massive, sweeping marks that I make over days using my whole body.

I'm yet to edit another film that I made inside the bamboo structure in Bangalore, on the terrace of my parents' house, which was very physical. I was painting on the bamboo walls with water and lime. The process involved applying layers and layers of lime and then drawing over it with water. The final piece will bring together the physicality of the space, or the architecture, the place itself, and the materials that I used, as well as the light. I see all these elements as equal players. There is an alchemy in how they come together and take form. And, of course, there is also the inner landscape that is very much present in the conversation with all of the physical components.

MM There is also the dimension of scale in your work that perhaps changes the relationship to space: you don't draw on a light box, you don't draw in a pencil-size scale, you don't draw on a tablet or on the screen. Your drawings are usually quite physical and require both arms, both legs, and practically the entire body to make a mark.

MB Yes, I think this has to do with building an intimate relationship with a space that we've touched upon earlier. Intimacy is not always smooth. There is a struggle to intimacy. There is a physicality to it. It is like a dance, and there is a rhythm to it. There is an animism to spaces: they are not just concrete walls. There is *life* there, and I want to explore that relationship: what happens in the interstice.

I dive into a space, dive into all the constraints, to see what comes out of that interaction, or that exchange.

The Stone was the first film in a long time that I actually drew quite small. When you're drawing big, you're inhabiting a space in a different way. But with *The Stone*, I was making it living in transition, in friends' homes, so I had to contain it. I couldn't inhabit those spaces in the same way, so I drew quite small, and then filmed the drawings on the windows of those homes.

Scale is very indicative of the time or the relationship with the place. Do I want to keep myself small there, or is it okay to be all over the wall?

When you're working on a very large scale, you have less control. And when you're not so much in control, things emerge, things that you could not have created otherwise. That is something that I'm fascinated with: the reward you get when you surrender control.

MM   In this book we are thinking about the future. I would like to ask you how do the ideas of the future play into your work? Is there any representation of what's to come in your practice?

MB   Sometimes, without me realising, my works have been a prediction of what's to come. Perhaps this is because I work very intuitively. For example, the film *Shifting Ground*, which I made in 2012 at the beginning of a very difficult time personally, was the beginning of the end of my marriage. I wasn't fully aware of it, but it was impending. This was playing out in my studio, yet I couldn't understand it. I just had to follow the work through and embrace the form it was taking.

In some ways I understand my work only in retrospect, looking back and realising what it was about. I think my work is a continuum of paying deep attention to the present moment.

Contributors

Adania Shibli (b. 1974, Palestine) writes fiction and non-fiction. Her latest novel *Tafsil Thanawi* (Beirut: Al-Adab, 2017, translated into English as *Minor Detail* published by Fitzcarraldo Editions/New Directions, 2020) was the finalist for the National Book Award 2020. She has been teaching part-time at Birzeit University, Palestine, and is a researcher in cultural studies and visual culture.

Alia Trabucco Zerán was born in Chile in 1983. Her debut novel *La Resta* (*The Remainder*) was shortlisted for the Man Booker International Prize and won the prize for Best Unpublished Literary Work awarded by the Chilean Council for the Arts. In 2019 she published *Las Homicidas* (*The Killers*), a non-fiction book that explores how iconic cases of women who kill challenge what society considers 'normal' in women. She lives between London and Santiago.

Alison Irvine is a novelist and non-fiction writer. Her first novel *This Road is Red* (Luath) was shortlisted for the 2011 Saltire First Book of the Year Award. Her second novel *Cat Step* (Dead Ink) was published in November 2020. She is the writer in the artist collective Recollective and a tutor on the Masters in Creative Writing at the University of Glasgow.

Bedwyr Williams lives and works in North Wales. His solo exhibitions include *The Institute of Things to Come*, Fondazione Sandretto Re Rebaudengo, Turin, 2017; *The Gulch*, The Curve, Barbican Art Centre, 2016; *The Starry Messenger*, Whitworth Art Gallery, Manchester, 2015; *Echt*, Tramway, Glasgow, 2014; *My Bad*, Ikon Gallery, Birmingham, 2012. In 2013 he represented Wales at the Venice Biennale and was shortlisted for the Artes Mundi Prize in 2016.

Ben Okri is a poet, novelist, and playwright. His novel *The Famished Road* won the Booker Prize in 1991. His works have been translated into twenty-six languages. His book *Astonishing the Gods* was chosen by the BBC as one of the most influential novels written over the last 300 years. His latest novel is *The Freedom Artist* and his latest volume of stories is *Prayer for the Living*, both published in 2019. A new collection of poems *A Fire in my Head* was published in January 2021.

Crystal Bennes is an American artist and writer based in Scotland. Her mixed media practice is grounded in long-term projects that foreground archival research, durational fieldwork and material experimentation. Her current project – the subject of an AHRC-funded practice-based PhD – investigates gendered representations of nature in the history of science and feminist critiques of physics. Her writing on architecture and design has appeared in international publications including *Icon*, *Frieze*, *Disegno* and *Metropolis*.

Jodie Azhar is the CEO and Game Director at Teazelcat Games, a studio focused on story-driven games. Prior to this, she spent a decade working as a technical artist at various game development studios, including as the Technical Art Director for the *Total War* franchise. She is an award-winning developer, was one of BAFTA's Breakthrough Brits of 2016, and is a founding member of the games diversity movement POC in Play.

Justinien Tribillon is an urbanist, writer, editor and curator, who works across different media and disciplines including social science, photography, architecture, and history. A tutor and PhD candidate at The Bartlett School of Planning, UCL, Justinien is co-founder and editor of *Migrant Journal*. Between 2017 and 2020, Justinien was Researcher then Associate Director for Europe at Theatrum Mundi. He has written for *The Guardian*, *MONU*, *The Architectural Review*, *Magnum*.

Marta Michalowska is a curator, producer, artist and writer based in London. She has recently completed her debut novel *Sketching in Ashes*, supported by Arts Council England through the Developing Your Creative Practice programme, and is currently writing her second one *A Tram to the Beach*, both exploring contested territories. Michalowska is Associate Director of Theatrum Mundi and Director of The Wapping Project.

Matthew Dooley is a cartoonist from the north-west of England. His debut graphic novel *Flake* won the 2020 Bollinger Everyman Wodehouse Prize for Comic Fiction, the first graphic novel to win the prize in its twenty-year history. When not drawing he likes playing lawn bowls and painting toy soldiers.

Meghana Bisineer (b. 1978) is an Indian-born animation artist, curator and educator. She works between London, UK, and Oakland, California. Her practice traverses artist collaborations, experimental film and installation across galleries, art spaces and festivals. Her films have been shown internationally. Since 2016, she has been Assistant Professor of Animation and Graduate Fine Arts at the California College of the Arts in San Francisco, USA.

Mona Kareem is the author of three poetry collections. She held fellowships and residencies with Princeton University, Poetry International, Arab-American National Museum, National Centre for Writing, and Forum Transregionale Studien. Kareem's English translation of Ashraf Fayadh's *Instructions Within* was nominated for the Best Translated Book Award in 2016. Her selected translations of Ra'ad Abdulqadir will be published by Ugly Duckling Presse in spring 2021. Her Arabic translation of Octavia Butler's *Kindred* was released in autumn 2020.

Natasha Lehrer's criticism and essays have appeared in *The Guardian*, *The Observer*, *Times Literary Supplement*, *The Nation* and *Fantastic Man*, among others. Her prizewinning translations include *Suite for Barbara Loden* by Nathalie Léger (winner of the 2017 Scott Moncrieff Translation Prize) and *Memories of Low Tide* by Chantal Thomas (shortlisted for the 2020 Scott Moncrieff Prize).

Nina Leger is a writer and an art critic. She lives between Paris and Marseille where she teaches art history at the Ecole des Beaux-Arts. Her critically acclaimed novel *Mise en Pièces* (Gallimard, 2017) won the Prix Anaïs Nin, and was published in English by Granta as *The Collection* (2019). Her other writings include texts for artists' books, exhibition catalogues and art history journals.

Sophie Hughes is a translator of Spanish and Latin American literature, including novels by Enrique Vila-Matas, Laia Jufresa and Rodrigo Hasbún. She has been shortlisted for the International Booker Prize twice, for *The Remainder* by Alia Trabucco Zerán in 2019, and *Hurricane Season* by Fernanda Melchor in 2020.

Sophie Mackintosh is a writer based in London. Her fiction, essays and poetry have been published by *Granta*, *The White Review*, *The New York Times* and *The Stinging Fly*, among others. Her debut novel *The Water Cure* was long-listed for the Man Booker Prize 2018, and her second novel *Blue Ticket* was published in 2020.

Acknowledgments

This book is the latest development in the project – Enactments – which we initiated in 2019 at Theatrum Mundi to connect ideas at the intersection of storytelling, architecture and urban planning. It has been nurtured by workshops, research and public programmes taking place in London, Paris and Prague. We would like to thank the participants and partner institutions, named below, who have contributed to this collective exploration over the past two years, and our current and former colleagues at Theatrum Mundi who contributed their time, expertise and ideas. We are indebted to everyone who engaged in conversations with us: pushing ideas of what narrative is and can be in the practices of designing and planning cities, and how we can negotiate the paths between the extremes of utopia and dystopia.

We would like to extend our thanks to Eelco van Welie of nai010 publishers who engaged with the project early on in its journey and gave us the opportunity to produce this book, the first in the upcoming series *Staging Cities*, a longer collaboration between Theatrum Mundi and nai010.

This book would not look so sharp and sleek without the designers at Atelier Dyakova. We would like to thank Sonya Dyakova, Tom Baber and Gabriella Voyias for working closely with us on shaping this first volume of *Staging Cities*.

This project would not be possible without Theatrum Mundi's board of trustees, as well as the funders who provide the invaluable support that makes our research and ideas thrive. We cannot thank them enough for their generosity and trust.

And last but not least we would like to thank friends and family who were there for us throughout the process of editing this book.

Gwenaëlle d'Aboville / Adesola Akinleye / Corina Angheloiu / Jodie Azhar / Gruia Bădescu / Jan Bažant / Crystal Bennes / John Bingham-Hall / Andrea Cetrulo / Jasmina Cibic / Emmanuelle Chiappone-Piriou / Cecily Chua / Ariel Davis / Jean-Baptiste Delafon / Pavel Drábek / David Enon / Imogen Free / Kate Harding / Alison Irvine / Elahe Karimnia / Meneesha Kellay / Fani Kostourou / Irena Lehkoživová / Nina Leger / Stéphanie Loyer / Sophie Mackintosh / David Malaud / Lou-Atessa Marcellin / Océane Ragoucy / Efrosini Protopapa / Jane Scarth / Christopher Ian Smith / Barbora Špičáková / Cécile Trémolières / Pierre-Alain Trévelo / Katerina Vídenová / Antoine Viger-Kohler / Beth Weinstein / Dork Zabunyan

TVK, Paris
The 2019 Prague Quadrennial of Performance Design and Space
VI PER Gallery, Prague
Whitechapel Gallery, London

www.theatrum-mundi.org/project/enactments/

Concrete & Ink: Storytelling and the Future of Architecture is the first volume in the series *Staging Cities*, which borrows from the toolbox of storytelling, choreography, and sound and lighting design to propose new approaches to questions faced by city-makers, published by Theatrum Mundi and nai010 publishers.

Theatrum Mundi
15A Clerkenwell Close
London EC1R 0AA
info@theatrum-mundi.org
www.theatrum-mundi.org

nai010 publishers
Tel +31 (0)10 2010133
Fax +31 (0)10 2010130
info@nai010.com
www.nai010.com

Series Editors
Marta Michalowska
John Bingham-Hall

Editors of This Issue
Marta Michalowska
Justinien Tribillon

Image Credits
pp. 49-60:
Matthew Dooley
pp. 112-116:
Bedwyr Williams
pp. 150-160:
Meghana Bisineer

Design
Atelier Dyakova, London

Copy Editing
Marta Michalowska

Proofreading
The Book Edit

Printing
Grafistar

Publisher
nai010 publishers

nai010 publishers is an internationally orientated publisher specialising in developing, producing and distributing books on architecture, visual arts and related disciplines.

nai010 books are available internationally at selected bookstores and from the following distribution partners:

North, South and Central America – Artbook | D.A.P., New York, USA, dap@dapinc.com

Rest of the world – Idea Books, Amsterdam, the Netherlands, idea@ideabooks.nl

For general questions, please contact nai010 publishers directly at sales@nai010.com or visit our website www.nai010.com for further information.

Printed and bound in the EU

ISBN 978-94-6208-616-6

NUR 648
BISAC ARC010000,
PERO11040